Motorbooks International Illustrated Buyer's Guide Series

Illustrated

BMW
Motorcycle
BUYER'S ★ GUIDE™

Stefan Knittel & Roland Slabon

Motorbooks International
Publishers & Wholesalers ®

First published in 1990 by Motorbooks International Publishers & Wholesalers, P O Box 2, 729 Prospect Avenue, Osceola, WI 54020 USA

The information in this book is true and complete to the best of our knowledge. All recommendations are made without any guarantee on the part of the author or publisher, who also disclaim any liability incurred in connection with the use of this data or specific details

We recognize that some words, model names and designations, for example, mentioned herein are the property of the trademark holder. We use them for identification purposes only. This is not an official publication

Motorbooks International books are also available at discounts in bulk quantity for industrial or sales-promotional use. For details write to Special Sales Manager at the Publisher's address

Library of Congress Cataloging-in-Publication Data
Knittel, Stefan.
  Illustrated BMW motorcycle buyer's guide / Stefan Knittel, Roland Slabon.
    p. cm. — (Motorbooks International illustrated buyer's guide series)
    ISBN 0-87938-404-2 (soft)
    1. BMW motorcycle—Purchasing. I. Slabon, Roland
  II. Title. III. Series.
  TL448.B18K65 1990   90-40949
  629.227′5—dc20   CIP

On the front cover: A BMW tourer and sports-tourer from the sixties and the eighties: a classic 1967 BMW R60/2 600 cc in BMW's traditional black with white pinstriping and an R100RS Motorsport, one of only some 200 Motorsport versions imported into the United States, wearing the white with red-and-blue pinstriping paint scheme. *Jeff Dean*

On the back cover: From drum brakes to ABS, pressed-steel frame to enclosed fiberglass bodywork, these two BMW siblings are separated by sixty years: a 1929 R11 Series I 750 cc sidevalve and a 1989 K1 1000 cc in-line four-cylinder superbike.

Printed and bound in the United States of America

Contents

Acknowledgments

BMW motorcycles were the dreams of my youth some twenty years ago. I rode over the fields on all sorts of two-stroke bikes, but always desired a BMW four-stroke—in particular, the R25/3 of our local postman.

My brother soon got a red and white R25, and we were quite happy with it for many years. The R60 of some time later was saved from becoming a chopper due only to a lack of money. A 1969 R75/5 became my first long-distance tourer in 1975. An R100RT took me to the Isle of Man in 1982, and a year later I was the first person outside of the factory to ride a K100.

This ride on the K100 is easily explained as I had to take photographs of the bike for use in my book, *BMW Motorrader: 65 Jahre Tradition und Innovationen* (Bleicher Verlag, 1988). Keeping in touch with what is going on at BMW has always presented me with an opportunity to ride a new model for a business trip on German autobahns or a road test on our Alpine roads here in Bavaria.

Knowing my background, Tim Parker of Motorbooks International invited me to write an Illustrated Buyer's Guide volume on BMW motorcycles. I agreed to the task.

The right sort of support came from BMW Munich, which provided me not only with every bit of information requested, but also nearly all the photographs. My ever-helpful friends Hans Sautter, who is BMW's capable motorcycle press officer, and Peter Zollner, who looks after the BMW archives, let me again search through their files and drawers.

Stefan Knittel
Dietramszell, Bavaria, Germany
January 1990

As editor and publisher of the *Vintage BMW Bulletin*, my involvement with BMW motorcycles, in particular those built prior to 1970, goes back to the very beginnings of the vintage BMW movement in the United States. After being asked by the Alabama founder of Vintage BMW Motorcycles Owners, Ltd. to take over as newsletter editor in 1973, I was forced not only to research and write about all of BMW's more desirable prewar and postwar models, but also to learn in no small measure just what it was that made BMW motorcycles so appealing.

In the past eighteen years, nearly three dozen motorcycles have ended up at one time or another, in various stages of disrepair, in my basement. I've been fortunate enough to keep six or seven of the very best, the most technically interesting and the most practical. Unfortunately, some of the better ones, such as several R12s, an R4 and an R71 were sold for one reason or another; yet the best still remain, including my favorite R12, which still gets used for a good run

5

now and then. As much as I regret selling my first "modern" BMW, a 1971 R50/5, which more than all the others taught me how to ride safely, if not altogether fast, I still cherish my older ones the most: the Earles-fork R50/2 for its practicality, the plunger-frame R68 and R67/2 for their sporting character and good looks, the pressed-steel R12 and R16 for their unique styling and technical innovation, and the R42 for its place in history, and because it ended up here with my wife Susan and I as a cherished wedding gift from a good friend in Belgium. All the others—the Hondas, Zündapps, Norton, NSU, even the Vincent—have come and gone. Only the BMWs remain, as does the friendship of the hundreds of BMW enthusiasts, who have become as much a part of this hobby for me as the restoration, enjoyment and use of vintage BMW motorcycles. Without their long-time involvement and support, the need for clubs and newsletters and books such as this would not have been so well-defined, nor so pleasant an undertaking.

Grateful thanks to all the friends who helped make this book possible. Your enthusiasm, assistance and expert advice are reflected on the pages of this book.

A huge debt is owed to Hans Fleischmann, former head of the BMW Archives in Munich, and to Dr. Helmut Krackowizer, for providing numerous rare and detailed photos. Richard Kahn sent us, over the years, literally cartons of historical material from the Butler & Smith files. Vintage Club members Oscar Fricke, Bill Kuhlman, Richard Sheckler, Tracy Baker, Toby Rosner and Jonathan Hayt, to name but a few, provided their photographic expertise over the years and gave a unique insight into what makes owning, riding and restoring a BMW so fascinating.

Technical advice and assistance were cheerfully provided by Robert Hellman, editor of *On the Level* and his technical editor "Oak" Okleshen. Their expertise in the realm of post-vintage BMWs was especially useful.

Many Vintage BMW Club members will recognize themselves and their machines on these pages. For this we must gratefully thank Marie Lacko who, with husband John (club secretary for over a decade), attended virtually all events since 1976, and who used her professional photographic talents to the fullest to capture on film what are probably the best BMWs to be found in the United States.

I know that there are probably hundreds of Vintage Club members I have overlooked. One not to be forgotten is Larry Sparber, whose grasp of details and whose penchant for authenticity have made him a judge both feared and respected at any BMW gathering. Bob Henig, through his almost clinical knowledge of parts and accessories, helped identify and photograph all those delightful items we all love to attach to our BMWs and sidecars.

Finally, a long-overdue thank you to good friend John Harper, who had the vision nearly twenty years ago to bring a few enthusiasts who loved old BMWs together, and who encouraged this writer to set a few words on paper and continue publishing, for what has now been almost twenty years, the *Vintage BMW Bulletin*, which he and Jeff Dean had started back in 1972.

Roland Slabon
Exeter, New Hampshire, USA
April 1990

Introduction

BMW motorcycles have always been first and foremost riders' machines. Only rarely are they looked upon as true collector items or investments, since even the older and rarer ones are still able to provide excellent service and reliable transportation when properly maintained. The bikes are certainly long lasting—some have been on the road for almost seventy years now—and although well-used, can still be purchased with confidence. This is probably the best reason for buying a BMW today.

BMWs have come into favor among collectors and investors only recently, although the BMW enthusiasts have put many miles on their black machines with the white pinstriping. The old bike hobby in general has now grown into a substantial movement, and the German flat twins and their single-cylinder offshoots are now coming into their own.

BMWs have remained in closely guarded company for a long while, and the reason may have been that to the eye of the man in the street, all BMWs looked the same—at least until the appearance of the K Series bikes in 1983. And to be honest, it is not easy to spot the differences between the models if you're not deeply involved in BMW history. There is the R51, R51/2 and R51/3—it can require an expert to tell what is what.

That is why the *Illustrated BMW Motorcycle Buyer's Guide* was conceived. There have been surprisingly few volumes written on the history of the famous German Bavarian Motor Works, and most are in the language of their Fatherland. The complete history would fill a large expensive tome and in-depth studies of each model might be too much for the reader as well as for the authors. There are numerous reprinted workshop manuals and spares lists available for that purpose.

The *Illustrated BMW Motorcycle Buyer's Guide* can be seen as somewhere in between, providing a survey of all the different models built by the factory from 1923 to the present day and pointing out the main differences. This, together with period photographs of the machines as well as of recently restored examples, may provide the most important information you will need before getting involved deeper in the tasks of searching, buying and restoring.

We tried to refrain from interjecting too much of a personal view, for there are widely different tastes and preferences, even in the world of old motorcycles. Living only twenty-five miles away from BMW headquarters does not neccessarily mean you automatically become a rabid enthusiast for the make. There have been BMWs we liked and there have been some we did not enjoy, but we did not want to influence the readers through our judgments. Even quoting from period reports may not be too good an idea, if the writer's view should be biased in any way. After all, the question is how you now feel about an R69S in today's world, and not how the writer felt in 1962. This is the reason why there are only a few top speed and no fuel consumption figures given. Is it really that important now, whether the R25/3 does 65 or 70 mph?

One thing about the performance figures has to be explained, however. The power output is shown in German DIN-PS, the official power rating in Germany. In the 1970s, higher figures were released for the US market based on the SAE horsepower rating method, but the engine specification did not change and therefore we kept to the German figures.

Ownership and prospects ratings

The other ratings in this book relate to the collector status of every BMW model mentioned. This is not altogether intended to be the guideline to collecting as personal pref-erences could lead anybody to a different opinion. It's intended to only give you an idea about what models are preferred over others. At the same time it gives an indication of the different price levels one may be expected to pay.

Regardless of how we may have rated a particular model, tastes can and do change. Don't set yourself up for later disappointment by limiting yourself to a particular model which may not be right for you, or for your budget. Go after what appeals to you, not because of its rating. Consider the machine an investment in pleasure first, and not just a two-wheeled Certificate of Deposit. After all, an over-restored collectible BMW that you cannot ride and that you are afraid to let others touch, soon becomes nothing more than a static display, which will give the owner pleasure only when it is finally sold at a profit.

★★★★★ Five-star models are the ones everybody seems to be after. They are the rarest from their period, but as rarity alone does not warrant high popularity, they are usually important in their technical specifications as well. Prices have been going up, so there may be little time to think twice when one should come up for sale.

★★★★ The four-star bracket is now expanding, due to increased demand for the limited number of motorcycles available. Prices are rising steadily and the ever-increasing expense of restoration will be justified by a subsequent increase in value.

★★★ Three stars are given to models considered to be of average value. There is not that much demand yet, but it may change. It might be a good idea to start with such a model and use it rather than regard it as an investment.

★★ Two-star motorcycles are the more common bikes, the least liked and least able to keep up with their value in the market, but still can be nice machines as day-to-day riders.

★ One-star motorcycles are the bikes no one wants. A one-star can be a long shot for the future. If this is the bike you want, you can probably buy it cheap.

Chapter 1

Flat Twins 1923–1930

Model	Years	Type	Rating
R32	1923–1926	500 cc sv	★★★★
R37	1925–1926	500 cc ohv	★★★★★
R42	1926–1928	500 cc sv	★★★★
R47	1927–1928	500 cc ohv	★★★★★
R52	1928–1929	500 cc sv	★★★★
R57	1928–1930	500 cc ohv	★★★★★
R62	1928–1929	750 cc sv	★★★★
R63	1928–1929	750 cc ohv	★★★★★

First incorporated on July 23, 1917, the Bayerische Motoren-Werke (Bavarian Motor Works, or simply BMW) held a prominent position in the development of engines for the German aircraft industry during World War I. Their masterpiece was a 226 hp six-cylinder overhead-camshaft engine with a massive 19.1 liter capacity. Engines of this kind were no longer in demand after the end of hostilities, however, and BMW was forced to find new markets with its smaller engines for trucks and boats. This smaller engine met with little success, so a new motorcycle engine was soon added to the program. Based on the design of the British Douglas, a 500 cc flat twin was chosen. The horizontally opposed cylinders were of the side-valve type with the valves lying on top of the barrels. With the two connecting rods having their journals spread at 180 degrees on the mainshaft, the pistons worked in opposite directions, hence the name Boxer was given to the engine layout.

With only 6.5 hp on tap, BMW's customers, including the Victoria motorcycle

The Bayern Klein-Motor M2B15 motorcycle engine of 1920–22. This was the first motorcycle engine produced by BMW, and was sold to other motorcycle manufacturers in Germany and Europe. *Vintage BMW Bulletin, Oscar Fricke*

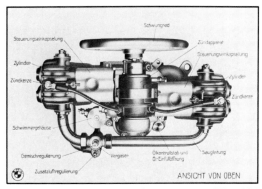

The M2B15 engine seen from the top. The 494 cc side-valve motor had an exposed flywheel and non-detachable cylinder heads. *Vintage BMW Bulletin, Oscar Fricke*

works at Nuremberg, Germany, soon asked for a more powerful version of the engine. But BMW had already made the decision to become a motorcycle manufacturer themselves and work had begun on a new style of modern touring motorcycle.

The flat-twin engine was used as a basis of the modern motorcycle but it was no longer

Victoria of Nuremberg was just one of many German motorcycle manufacturers to use the BMW proprietary engine, most of whom usually mounted the M2B15 motor front-to-aft with either belt or chain final drive.

mounted longitudinally in the frame. There had been problems with the longitudinally mounted engine as it was set too high in the frame because of the space needed for a gearbox; the wheelbase then grew too long and the cylinders did not get an equal amount of cooling. Turning the engine 90 degrees seemed to be the right idea, with the cylinders set across the frame; Sopwith's ABC motorcycle in England had set the pattern some years earlier. The outside flywheel was used to incorporate a clutch, and a three-speed gearbox was bolted directly to the elongated crankcases that housed the clutch to give a clean, compact-looking unit. Instead of using a bevel drive to a sprocket for a chain-driven rear wheel, BMW looked to the Belgian FN four-cylinder motorcycle and chose a straight shaft drive to the rear wheel. There, a pinion drove the crown wheel fitted to the axle. The rear drive was all covered in a neat aluminum-alloy housing.

It was obvious that a new frame design was needed to carry the engine and gearbox unit; the traditional bicycle-type diamond frame no longer seemed suitable. A twin-loop frame was therefore constructed from

The first BMW motorcycle was the R32, introduced in 1923. Seen here is the Series II R32, which, while still using a dummy-rim rear brake, has now been fitted with a small internal expanding-shoe front brake.

two steel tubes running down off of the steering head and curving under the engine, the frame being bolted together with cast footboards between the parallel tubes. From there the tubes ran on both sides of the rear wheel to the axle mount; the frame made a full loop on the left side whereas on the drive side, the crown-wheel housing bridged the gap to the top tube. Again parallel and inclined towards the ends, the tubes ran up to the steering head. To strengthen the frame, two short cross tubes were welded in between the main tubes on their top as well as the bottom in the space ahead of the rear wheel. Another vertical tube linked those braces, and the saddle was bolted to the top end of this tube. The front fork setup, with the wheel suspended from trailing links and springing by leaf springs from under the steering head, closely followed the pattern of the Indian motorcycle forks of the time.

The model was named the R32; the R stood for Rad, which means cycle, as opposed to the letter M for motor. The R32 was available beginning at the end of 1923. It was rather expensive but the quality of workmanship, the modern design and a high-

quality finish of the many alloy castings as well as the deep black paint with double pin-striping in white attracted a lot of interest. During 1924 no less than 1,500 R32 motor-

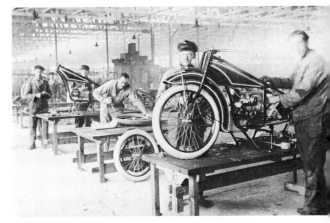

Early BMW motorcycle production in 1923–24. Seen here is the Series I R32, recognized by the lack of a front brake. Only a handful of proto-type R32s were built in 1923, and most of the R32s found in collections today are the later 1924–25 models.

An original factory photograph, from which the catalog photos were retouched. Here the R32 is fitted with the optional Bosch lighting system and horn, and a sprung pillion saddle.

Year and model	1923-1926 R32
Engine	Side-valve flat twin
Bore and stroke	68x68 mm
Displacement	494 cc
Horsepower	8.5 PS at 3300 rpm
Carburetion	Single BMW two-lever type, 22 mm
Ignition	Bosch magneto
Lubrication	Wet sump
Gearbox	Three-speed, hand actuated
Clutch	Single disc, dry
Frame	Twin tube
Suspension	Leading-link leaf-sprung front forks; rigid rear
Brakes	1923-24 no front brake, drum brake thereafter V-block on dummy belt rim at the rear wheel
Wheels and tires	20 in. wheels; 26x3 in. beaded-edge tires
Wheelbase	54.3 in.
Weight	265 lb. dry
Seat height	28.3 in.
Top speed	57 mph

Frontal view of the R37 showing the new enclosed overhead-valve cylinder heads. The twin levers on top of the handlebars are for throttle and mixture. The single small lever is for magneto spark advance and retard.

Riding a 1923 R32

It could have been no better coincidence. My first ride on BMW's first motorcycle came exactly sixty years after it was first shown to the public—and it was while taking the very first photographs of the K100, some weeks before it was shown to the world as a new BMW motorcycle design. Against today's models the R32 looks more like a moped, but at the same time distinctively different from the contemporary single-cylinder models and V-twins of the early 1920s.

A compact engine and gearbox unit dominates the motorcycle, mounted low in the twin-loop frame. The peculiar double-barrel carburetor of BMW's own design seems to be incorporated in the main casting, but it is bolted to an extension behind the flywheel housing and draws its intake air from there. The float chamber is on the other end where the intake would be expected. Turning on the petrol, tickling the float and positioning the two levers on the right-hand side of the handlebars are the necessary preparations prior to starting the engine. The combined levers are needed to adjust the two throttle valves in the carburetor in the way of a twin-stage control.

A few prods on the left-side kickstarter bring the flat twin to life. The idle speed is controlled by the two levers that can be left in any position as there are no return springs. Another control lever on the left-hand side of the handlebars is used for the advance mechanism on the magneto. Retarding the ignition timing makes starting easier even on a low-compression engine like this, and advancing it again immediately changes the sound of the engine. And what a lot of sounds there are. Most prominent is the action of the valves that work under detachable alloy covers on top of the cylinder barrels. A low tone is emitted from the stubby exhausts under the footboards.

Engaging the first gear by bringing the long lever into the top notch in its gate on the right-hand side of the tank also adds gear whine to the engine noise, but after slowly releasing the clutch the BMW makes a sudden move forwards. The riding position is dictated by a low seat, wide handlebars and the footboards. The sloping frame top with the underslung tank is too low and narrow to allow a firm knee grip, and even on the low saddle one feels perched on top of the vehicle.

While on the move, the valve noise changes into a loud whirr only slowing down when a gear change is made, which itself is accompanied by the all too familiar crunching sound from the teeth of the pinions. The ride seems to be stable and secure until the first ripples or small holes appear in the road surface, which the leaf springs of the front forks do not seem to heed. The rear wheel is unsprung, but it seems that the front one does not get much suspension travel either. The reason for wide handlebars allowing a firm grip is therefore easily explained.

Being aware of the fact that a side-valve 500 of those days was not very powerful compared to later ohv designs, the BMW R32 feels flat in its power delivery. The 8.5 PS at 3300 rpm may be a valid figure.

There is no real vibration to be felt in comparison to a single or V-twin, but the engine lacks their characteristically direct feel of real power. The biggest problem is getting used to the mechanical noise. There is an initial hesitation to open up the throttle too much, as one feels reluctant to overrev the engine. However, it will not fall apart, and will even run up to about 55 mph, but it takes time to get used to the way it does its job.

There are quite a few advantages that made the BMW superior to its competitors. Not only did the quality of the workmanship lead to greater reliability, but so did the compact design with enclosed valve gear and oil lines resulting in no exposed lubricated parts. There was no primary chain and only a thin shaft that drove the rear wheel, again with no grease flying around, and not prone to collect dirt from the road. The relative smoothness of the engine contributed to untiring travels at the low speed in those days, and the unnerving noise at 50 mph was hardly ever experienced.

Another surprise was the brakes. On the front wheel a small belt rim drives the speedometer, but there is a second V-block on a dummy belt rim at the rear wheel actuated by the inverted handlebar lever on the right. This one is not very effective as opposed to the clever design of the foot-operated main V-block. It has a long rubbing surface, divided into two parts with a pivot in the center, and when the foot lever is pressed down gently only the first half of the brakeshoe rubs into the rim, but with more pressure applied the other half comes into play. The result is a reasonably powerful brake providing good control of the action through a primitive form of self-servo effect.

The first BMW shares one characteristic in common with all other BMWs up to the present day: one has to get used to the different character of the flat-twin models from Germany, but after that they can be enjoyed as reliable and unassuming motorcycles for all sorts of travel.

cycles were built at the Munich factory and the standard layout for BMW motorcycles has never changed since: crankshaft, clutch, gearbox and driveshaft to the rear wheel mounted in line within a twin-tube frame.

New for the 1925 models was an internal-expanding drum brake for the front wheel where before there had been only a drive pulley for the speedometer belt. A speedometer and electric lights were available at extra cost.

Also new for the 1925 was a sports version, the R37, which made its debut in several races fielded by a team of BMW factory riders. Basically the same motorcycle as the R32, the R37 had new cylinder barrels turned from a billet of steel and detachable aluminum-alloy cylinder heads with overhead valves under a large oval cover. Fed by a special BMW carburetor with three slides, a rather conservative 16 PS at 4000 rpm was noted in the official catalog.

Alongside the limited-production R37, the first single-cylinder BMW was shown in 1925. Before the end of the year a redesigned touring twin, the R42, appeared in the catalog in addition to the R32, which it was to replace in 1926. The R42 had new cylinders with the cooling fins set across, and not along the length of the barrel as before. The flat heads were now detachable and made in alloy in a sort of two-level design that afforded perfect heat dissipation. The frame was redesigned as well, with the downtubes at the front no longer turned inwards to clear the front wheel, and with the engine set back a bit and the saddle tube curved along the rear fender. The reason for this was to achieve a better weight distribution. Also new was the rear brake with two

Beginning in 1925, the overhead-valve R37 soon became a popular competition model. The one seen here, without any electrical accessories, belonged to factory rider Franz Bieber.

The improved side-valve touring model, designated the R42, had a more powerful engine and new detachable cylinder heads, as well as a driveshaft brake, a redesigned three-speed gearbox incorporating a speedometer drive and a single-leaf front spring. Note that electrical accessories were still optional extras.

brakeshoes contracting onto a small drum on the driveshaft right behind the gearbox; the rear drum was heel-operated by a small lever. The former dummy belt rim brake on the R32 and R37 looked out of place on a shaft-driven model.

The R37 gave way to the updated R47 during 1927, which had the same new chassis as its side-valve stablemate, the R42. The ohv engine was not solely designed for racing purposes, and it therefore became both cheaper and more widely available. Steel barrels were no longer used as the production of cast-iron ones was more cost effective. The standard BMW carburetor with throttle and air slides also replaced the earlier tricky three-slide instrument. The updated engine could easily be recognized by the central bolt holding on the valve cover. Both models no longer used double leaf springs on the front forks and gained a cast-in sidecar mount on the rear-wheel-drive housing. Also new was a factory-fitted speedometer, mounted in a hole in the gas tank in front of the filler cap.

Meanwhile, BMW as a whole was doing quite well. The Munich factory had grown considerably as aircraft engines were once again increasingly in demand. At the same time, motorcycle production rose from 1,500 units in 1924 to nearly 5,000 by 1928.

In addition to the two 500 cc models, larger 750 cc versions made their first appearance in the BMW program during 1928. These were not merely overbored 500 cc engines, but were part of yet another series of changes also applied to the other engines. First, the former one-piece crankshaft gave way to a built-up press-fit crankshaft with the split big-ends on the connecting rods no longer required. Piston stroke was limited to two sizes: 78 mm for the side-valve engines and 68 mm for the sporting ohvs. Mated to their respective cylinder bores, this led to characteristic dimensions for each engine. The R52 side-valve 500 cc became a long-stroke motor with a bore and stroke of 63x78 mm, the ohv R57 500 cc was a square 68x68 mm, as was the R62 side-valve 750 cc with 78x78 mm. A rather modern short-stroke 750 cc was the ohv R63 with an 83 mm bore mated to the 68 mm stroke.

The mounting of the side-valve cylinder heads was again changed, and all models were now supplied with magneto-generator electrics as standard equipment. The Bosch

With the R47, the overhead-valve BMW became more widely available, but it still remained a dream for most motorcyclists. It was basically an R42 fitted with pushrods and overhead-valve cylinder heads.

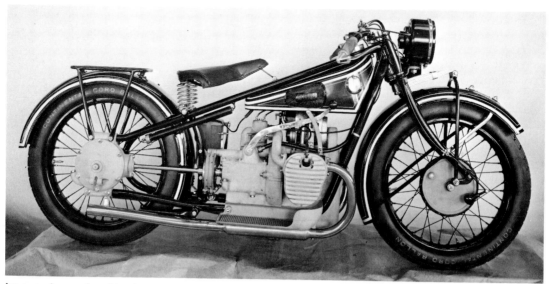

An even larger front brake, optional knee grips and revised cylinder heads distinguished this R52 from the earlier R42. It also had a relocated shift quadrant, and by this time electrical lighting was generally the rule.

electric lights were priced as extras in the catalog but from 1928 every BMW came fully equipped. A strengthened three-speed gearbox was introduced with the new engines, with the long hand-change lever now fitted to its top and no longer to the engine. The kickstart now had to be kicked to the side, and the mufflers beneath the footboards expanded into long tailpipes, soon to be supplemented by fishtail mufflers. And finally the brake drum at the front wheel was enlarged from 150 to 200 mm in diameter.

The power output for the 500 cc engines stayed at 12 PS at 3400 rpm for the R52 and 18 PS at 4000 rpm for the R57. Similarly, the side-valve 750 cc gave 18 PS at 3400 rpm and the top-of-the-range ohv R63 was conservatively rated with 24 PS at 4000 rpm. Even more modesty was shown with the official top speed announcement of 75 mph for the R63. In 1929, Ernst Henne's first motorcycle world speed record of 133.8 mph on an R63 fitted with a supercharger showed the potential of the Munich boxer engines.

A common sight on the roads as well as on the racetracks for quite some years, the first generation of BMW motorcycles gave way to all-new concepts at the end of 1929 after 22,000 of these flat-twin models, with the characteristic triangular gas tank mounted between the engine and the frame top tubes, had been produced.

Prospects

Surprisingly high production and thriving export sales by BMW from the early days on did not leave too many surviving models.

A fully equipped R57 from 1929 with the magneto-generator lighting set from Bosch. Other than having an overhead-valve engine, its layout was the same as the R52.

16

There are always one or two available in Germany but rarely anywhere else. The ones that come onto the market are either incomplete restoration projects or increasingly expensive restored examples.

In recent years remanufactured spares have become available in Germany, including exhaust systems, footboards, headlamps and piston sets. It is, however, still difficult to tackle an incomplete example. As most of these BMWs would have seen a long active service life in the hands of numerous owners, well-worn components, especially in the engine-gearbox-rear-drive area, should be expected. Extensive and costly repair jobs have to be considered.

There seem to be quite a number of early model BMWs around in Germany which do look the part with new nickel and paint but are hardly runners at all. As one can imagine, these models do command a high reputation in Germany notwithstanding their actual running capabilities. But the scene is changing and more machines are beginning to be used on the roads once again, even if it is only for a club run.

Year and model	1928–1930 R57
Engine	Overhead-valve flat twin
Bore and stroke	68x68 mm
Displacement	494 cc
Horsepower	18 PS at 4000 rpm
Carburetion	Single BMW two-lever type, 22 mm
Ignition	Bosch magneto
Lubrication	Wet sump
Gearbox	Three-speed, hand actuated
Clutch	Single disc, dry
Frame	Twin tube
Suspension	Leading-link leaf-sprung front forks; rigid rear
Brakes	Drum brake at the front wheel; contracting band on driveshaft drum
Wheels and tires	19 in. wheels; 26x3.5 in. wired-on tires
Wheelbase	55 in.
Weight	330 lb. dry
Seat height	28.3 in.
Top speed	72 mph

Ratings

From a historic value alone all models should be solid five-star prospects, but this has recently shifted. Once coveted as the first BMW motorcycle, the R32 has now lost out a bit against the overhead-valve models. The reason is quite simple. The R32 is not

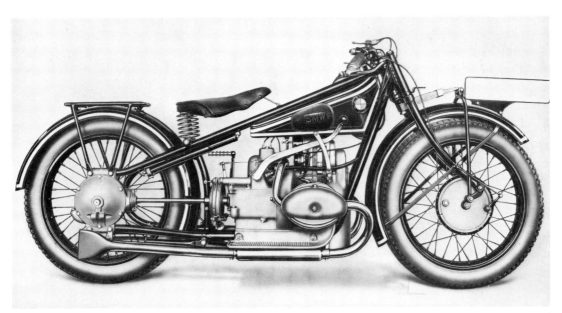

The 750 cc R63 had wider-bore barrels and larger cylinder heads. In this side view, the only difference from the R57 is the different bend of the intake manifold.

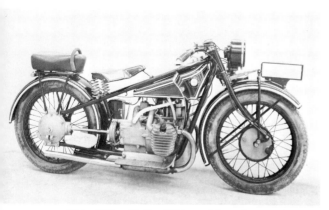

This R62 with the 750 cc side-valve engine has the optional legshields and a pillion seat fitted. The difference from the 500 cc R52 engine is only in the size of the cylinder heads.

too practical as a vintage motorcycle when it comes time to ride. It is not very powerful and feels rather top-heavy in the handling department. Together with the other side-valvers—the R42, R52 and R62, which are all superior in that respect—the R32 seems to be limited to a four-star rating.

Top marks definitely go to the R37, the ultra-rare first sporting BMW of which only a handful of genuine examples are known to exist in Germany.

Five stars go to the R47, R57 and R63 as well, with the latter the most interesting of the trio due to its 750 cc displacement.

You can sometimes still find them like this, even today! This 1926 R42 survived World War II's destruction and scrap metal drives, and was offered for sale by its West Berlin owner for $2,000 back in 1974. To his everlasting regret, Roland Slabon passed up the opportunity to buy it. *Vintage BMW Bulletin, Hans Kaiser*

In this left-side view of the same West Berlin R42, the unusual rearward-swinging kickstart and the tiny door in the gearbox that houses the toolkit are visible. Although the little 500 cc R42 produced only 12 PS at 3400 rpm, its weight of only 277 lb. gave it spritely performance when compared to its contemporaries. *Vintage BMW Bulletin, Hans Kaiser*

Chapter 2

Flat Twins 1929–1944

Model	Years	Type	Rating
R11	1929–1934	750 cc sv	★★★★
R16	1929–1934	750 cc ohv	★★★★
R12	1935–1942	750 cc sv	★★★★
R17	1935–1937	750 cc ohv	★★★★★
R5	1936–1937	500 cc ohv	★★★★★
R6	1937	600 cc sv	★★★★
R51	1938–1940	500 cc ohv	★★★★
R61	1938–1941	600 cc sv	★★★★
R71	1938–1941	750 cc sv	★★★★
R66	1938–1941	600 cc ohv	★★★★★
R75	1941–1944	750 cc ohv	★★★★★

It came as a big surprise for both buyers and competing manufacturers when BMW released two further new models at the Motor Cycle Show in London in November 1928. At a time when the four-model program was going from strength to strength in sales, there seemed to be little reason for increasing the range.

The two 750 cc models received new frames to combat increasing customer complaints about collapsing front forks and other frame fractures in different areas that occurred especially on the R62s during sidecar duties. It escalated to a point which needed to be dealt with, especially if more machines could thereby be sold to military and police forces. Development work on the standard frames had failed so far, as the problems were always traced back to the welding at the joints of the curved, and therefore unduly stressed, tubes. The only solution seemed to be a radical change to the frame design, but BMW chose a different route by keeping the layout of the chassis, yet supplanting the weak tubes with pressed steel. Motorcycle frames made from steel pressings were already known, mostly with smaller-capacity models from the early 1920s on. The new BMW frame, however, was of a new design never before seen, with its two loops in one pressing each, joined by cross-members and welded together at the front to embrace the steering-head stock. Gusseting was incorporated into the pressing near the steering head as well. The front forks remained a trailing-link pattern with the main beams made out of pressed steel. Together with the valanced front mudguard and the gas tank nearly hidden within the hefty frame rails and side pressings, the new chassis looked ready to handle the tough jobs often given a commercial or military sidecar outfit.

German industrial art at its best. This rendering of an R6 side-valve engine graced the cover of a 1937 BMW sales brochure.

Named the R11 with the side-valve engine and R16 with the ohv engine, the new 750s appeared in the new catalogs at the beginning of 1929, although only a handful actually left the factory later in the year. This delay was due to problems with the front forks and some other teething troubles, and while a redesign of the front end was done, the tubular-framed R62 and R63 remained in production. It was not until autumn 1929 that the next year's program actually saw the changeover to the pressed-steel models with engines unmodified from their predecessors.

The new motorcycles sold well enough, but the worsening economic situation after the Wall Street Crash led to a drop in production during 1932 and 1933. Their technical development, however, did not slow down, and there were a number of modifications on the R11 and R16 models from one year to the next. When Bosch changed their headlamp design from the drum type to a more modern cup shape in 1930, BMW also added a stronger thrust bearing to the twin-disc clutch, wider brake shoes with four ribs instead of three on the driveshaft and an additional bearing in the rear drive. New carburetors led to the Series III specification in 1932, although the series distinction was only used for internal factory purposes. The side-valve R11 also received a three-jet carburetor from Sum of Berlin with pre-heated secondary air drawn through a small tube on each side from the exhaust manifold. On the R16, the single BMW carburetor gave way to two Amal needle-jet carburetors, made under British license by Fischer in Frankfurt, fitted directly to the inlet stubs on each cylinder head. These 1 in. carburetors were responsible for a considerable increase in the official power figure, to 33 PS at 4000 rpm, which seemed a bit more exciting than the lowly 25 PS of the past.

More changes followed in 1933 with the Series IV models, which had new big-end bearings with single-row caged roller bearings versus the twin-row rollers used before and a new gear-change mechanism working in a gate covered by the knee-grip rubber on the right-hand side. A saddle with tension springs was also new for that year.

The main modification for the 1934 Series V models was not easily spotted but an experienced rider would have heard it. The timing gears that drove the camshaft and the magneto-generator from the front end of the crankshaft added a lot of whine to the normal engine noises, and when in an effort to quiet the machines new effective fishtail

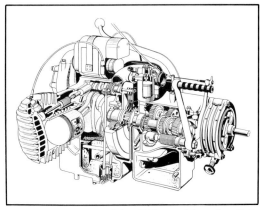

A sectioned view of the 750 cc side-valve flat-twin motor of the BMW R11. The horizontal Sum carburetor and the wide brakeshoe on the driveshaft identify this as a Series III engine from 1931. This engine design remained basically unchanged through 1942, when the last R12s were still being produced for the military. The large rectangular plate on the side of the gearbox is the toolbox door.

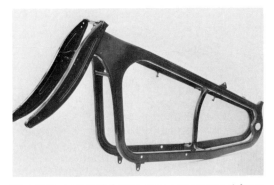

The R11 and R16 frame was constructed from two steel pressings welded together. The fork blades were also made in pressed steel. All in all, it made for a very rigid and robust frame, ideally suited to the attachment of a sidecar.

A Series I R11 from 1929 with the old type of Bosch headlamp and the BMW carburetor. Spotting detail differences between the five series of the R11 and R16 models requires a trained eye, and lots of background reading. Even then some clues such as headlamp and tailpipe design overlapped each other.

A pressed-steel frame, girder forks, leaf springs and factory legshields all combine to make this original, running and unrestored 750 cc sidevalve R11 of 1931 a frequent favorite at United States Vintage Club gatherings. *Vintage BMW Bulletin, Rich Sheckler*

mufflers were put into use, something had to be done. Thus, a roller chain replaced the timing gears driving the camshaft from 1934 on. Finally the R11 received the two Amal carburetors like its stablemate, producing 20

Year and model	1929-1934 R16
Engine	Overhead-valve flat twin
Bore and stroke	83x68 mm
Displacement	735 cc
Horsepower	25 PS at 6000 rpm, 1929-1931; 33 PS at 5000 rpm, 1932-1934
Carburetion	Single BMW three-jet type, 26 mm; twin Amals from 1932, 25 mm
Ignition	Bosch magneto-generator
Lubrication	Wet sump
Gearbox	Three-speed, hand actuated
Clutch	Single disc, dry
Frame	Twin loop pressed-steel section
Suspension	Leading-link leaf-sprung front; rigid rear
Brakes	Drum brake at the front wheel; contracting band on driveshaft drum
Wheels and tires	19 in. wheels; 26x3.5 in. tires
Wheelbase	54.3 in.
Weight	364 lb.
Seat height	27.5 in.
Top speed	75 mph

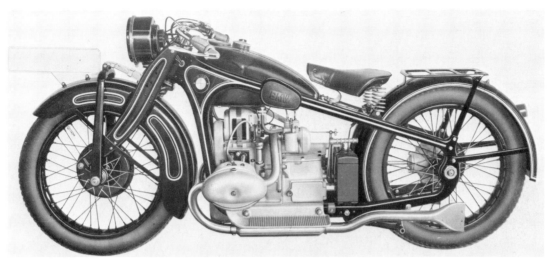

An ohv R16 Series I from 1929 with the same engine as the 750 cc R63 from the year before.

The toolbox door below the gearbox is clearly visible.

In 1930 the Series II R16 used the new headlamp and an additional bearing housing at the rear-wheel drive. Also seen here is a horn, missing on the photo of the 1929 R16, as well as the new twistgrip throttle.

Of the many prototype BMWs to have seen the light of day only to wither on the vine, few can match the grace and elegance of this R7, an engineering exercise by Alfred Boening, who later collaborated in the design of the famous R75 of 1941–45. The R7, with probably the ultimate in pressed steel frames, must have made quite a hit in 1934, for it was but a year later that the identical fender, forks and brake, plus a similar saddle and rear fender, appeared on the R12 and R17, both of which were offered to the public as 1936 models. Alas, for whatever the reasons, the R7, like so many others, was never to be.

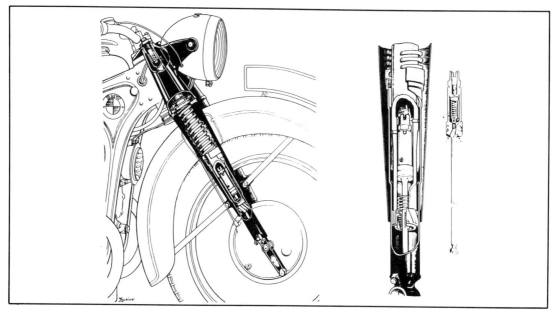

BMW introduced the first oil-damped telescopic front forks to the motorcycling world in 1935.

First seen on the R7 prototype, the forks entered into production with the R12 and R17 models.

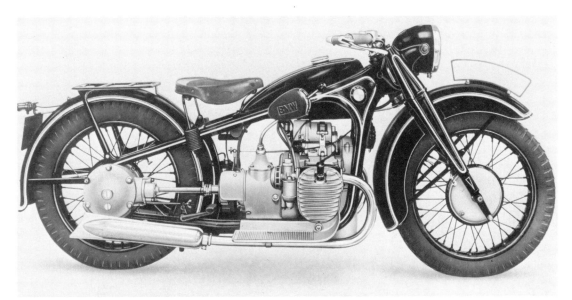

Telescopic forks and a four-speed gearbox converted the R11 into the R12. This is the rarer twin-carburetor model of 1935 that produced 20 PS. The great majority of the more than 36,000 R12s built had a single Sum carburetor and two pre-heater pipes running back to the manifold from the exhaust ports.

The single-carburetor R12 as it was produced exclusively for the German Wehrmacht between 1938 and 1942. Note the footrests instead of the alloy footboards, the pre-heater pipes and the crude military fenders, which were designed to shed mud and snow much better than those beautifully valanced and scalloped art deco fenders of the road model. The steel sidecar mounting ball bolted to the cast-alloy rear-drive casing.

PS at 3400 rpm. Both models could be had with coil ignition instead of the magneto on special order.

With the help of a good choice of models from the 200 cc and 400 cc singles to the well-proven big twins, BMW was successful as never before. Between 1933 and 1934, production more than doubled from 4,734 to

The sports model R17 was the most expensive German motorcycle of its day. Only 436 were produced during 1935–37, and with 33 PS available at 5000 rpm, it's still possible to keep up with today's highway traffic.

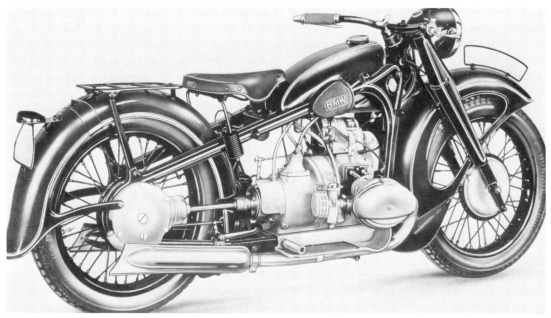

In 1936 the 750s received the sweeping fenders, lending the rare R17 an even more exotic image.

Even the sedate R12 benefited from this styling exercise.

9,689 motorcycles; in addition there were 8,322 BMW cars made at the Eisenach factory acquired at the end of 1928.

A bright future seemed assured at the Berlin Motor Show in February 1935 when two new 750 flat twins were shown in an updated form. A striking feature was the new front forks, the first telescopics in a modern style incorporating hydraulic damping action, a major advance over the then-common girder forks with their friction dampers. The pressed-steel frame and the engines remained largely unchanged, and only the crankshafts were beefed up. There was also a new gearbox with four speeds, still changed by hand through the gate on the right-hand side. A conventional drum brake for the rear wheel made the wheel interchangeable with the front one where the brake lever was now mounted inside the alloy brake plate. The latter was anchored to the fork leg by an elongation of the stanchion below the axle.

These robust BMWs had put on more weight with 407 lb. dry but this did not deter enthusiastic buyers throughout the world, and now other manufacturers were follow-

Riding a 1936 R12

This particular R12, a civilian model, was assembled in 1936 and apparently came to the United States in 1938, being imported from Germany by the first American owner. Some documentation exists indicating contact with BMW during the war years, when an attempt was made to procure parts. The factory's letter, read and resealed by censors from both sides, referred the owner to a dealer in Argentina, as parts were in understandably short supply in Germany at that time.

After the war the R12 was set aside, and it rested at various times inside and outside of a barn in New Hampshire. It was then made to run again, was stolen and recovered in Maine. During this episode, the original front fender was discarded by the thief to alter the R12's appearance and was replaced by a later-version BMW fender. The R12 then ended up, still running but unrestored, in Massachusetts, where it then changed hands twice, being fully restored by the most recent owner. Author Roland Slabon acquired the R12 in the spring of 1973 from the estate of her late owner in Salem, Massachusetts. It took another eight years and the help of friends in Germany and Belgium before a correct replacement front fender was finally located and restored to match the rest of the machine.

Upon initial encounter, the R12 appears sinister, lurking long, black and low on the centerstand, the rear wheel a full inch off the ground. Items usually plated, such as handlebars, spokes and rims, are done in gleaming lacquer. A shift lever, in a gated quadrant, curves out of an automotive-type gearbox on the right side of the tank. A plated driveshaft, fully as thick as one's thumb, points back to a solidly mounted rear drive, flanked by two beautifully finned mufflers. One tiny carburetor hides under the tank and feeds its mixture to the engine via two long curved cast manifolds, which are in turn preheated by two chrome tubes running back from the exhaust ports. A strange round plate on the left side of the transmission drops down to reveal an enormous cavern, which once housed a tool kit, now forever lost.

This 1936 R12 is the single-carburetor 745 cc side-valve version, producing 18 PS at 3400 rpm. The twin-carburetor model put out 20 PS at 4000 rpm. Top speed was 69 and 75 mph, respectively. The R12 and its sibling, the R17, were the first BMWs with oil-dampened telescopic front forks, and the R12 was produced from 1935 to 1942.

The key, with its familiar spike, plugs into the headlight shell that houses the speedometer, moved there from the gas tank for the first time with the R12 and R17 models. Then, open the tap, tickle the float, briefly turn on the choking screw on the carburetor, retard the spark from the left grip, crack open the throttle on the right grip, put the lever in neutral in the H-patterned gate and tromp down on the kickstarter. The engine fires at once and if you don't get the two handgrips confused, it settles down to a quiet, but busy, idle. The rear wheel, off the ground, spins merrily along, even in neutral, indicating some need for adjustment.

While everything is warming up, look inside the tank, which contains a wire-screen tube with little numbered tabs. The first tab visible above the fuel surface tells you how many liters of gas remain in the tank. Very clever.

Now, rock off the centerstand, pull in the clutch, put the lever in first—marked 1 on the

At speed on the 1936 750 cc side-valve R12. The avant-garde art deco styling of the R12 gives the impression that there are more than 18 PS housed within the 750 cc crankcase. *BMW of North America, Greg Jarem*

gate—crank the throttle toward you, the spark away from you, using all your hands and wishing you had just one more, then let out the clutch and pull away. Shifting is a series of lurches at first, but the engine thrives on low revs and just lugs along.

One quickly learns, and forever remembers, to never let out the clutch after a gear change until the right hand is firmly back on the throttle grip. The left foot is useless, resting idle on the floorboard, while the right must be lifted up and back to reach the rear brake pedal. Brakes are marginal. The revolutionary (for 1935) telescopic forks respond as if they were filled with molasses, and fork travel is minimal. The ride is bouncy but this is mainly due to nervous reaction and a softly sprung seat.

The R12 heels over nicely in the turns and really tracks well on the straight, smooth stretches proving once again that this BMW was, and is, a superb touring machine.

Year and model	1935–1942 R12
Engine	Side-valve flat twin
Bore and stroke	78x78 mm
Displacement	745 cc
Horsepower	18 PS at 3400 rpm; 20 PS at 4000 rpm, twin-carburetor version
Carburetion	Single Sum three-jet, 25 mm; twin Amals, 26 mm, optional
Ignition	Coil; magneto optional
Lubrication	Wet sump
Gearbox	Four-speed, hand actuated
Clutch	Twin-disc, dry
Frame	Twin loop pressed-steel section
Suspension	Telescopic front forks; rigid rear
Brakes	Drum brakes front and rear
Wheels and tires	3.50x19 in.
Wheelbase	54.3 in.
Weight	408 lb.
Seat height	27.5 in.
Top speed	66 mph

ing the pattern of the Munich engineers with similar pressed-steel frames and flat-twin engines. A direct competitor situated not far away from the Bavarian capital, was Zündapp from Nuremberg, which had started a complete line with pressed-steel frames from a 200 cc two-stroke single to an 800 cc flat-four including flat-twins of 500 and 600 cc. In France the aircraft engine company Gnome-Rhone had started to build similar motorcycles as early as 1931. Still, the BMW R12, as the side-valve 750 cc version was named, attracted a lot of response due to an attractive price. In Germany it was sold at 1630 Reichsmark which was 480 Marks more than the 400 cc single R4 and 410 Marks below the sporting ohv 750, designated as the R17.

An even more spectacular BMW made its debut later in 1935: the new works racer with a supercharged 500 cc engine. The Kompressor had first been used on record-breaking machines and since 1929, on the factory race bikes as well. But the new engine was no longer a slightly modified pushrod ohv unit. Instead, a wholly new concept with shaft-and-bevel-driven twin overhead camshafts on each cylinder head was chosen. Steel tubing was used for the frame, this time joined together by the new process of electric-arc welding. The only familiar sights on this motorcycle were the

Boxer layout of the engine and the telescopic front forks similar to the R12 and R17.

High hopes that a similar model would be available to the public were never realized, but the centerpiece at the Berlin Motor Show in February 1936 was a completely new BMW which did not look all that different from the racer at first glance. The design of the frame was similar, with the same sort of cold-drawn conical tubing with oval section, all of it electric-arc welded. The telescopic front forks had been further developed with external damping adjustment. The shapely gas tank was also used, and it gained a tool compartment, which was sunk into the top.

The engine was a new 500 cc Boxer with pushrod and rocker valve mechanism built around a one-piece crankcase where the crankshaft had to be inserted from the front, together with a front casting that held the front main bearing. Two chain-driven camshafts were mounted on top of the crankshaft to allow for shorter tappets and pushrods in order to make them lighter and able to withstand much greater loads at higher rpm. On the cylinder heads, cast-in rocker supports and double hairpin valve springs also showed the factory's efforts at attaining increased strength. Under a bulbous front

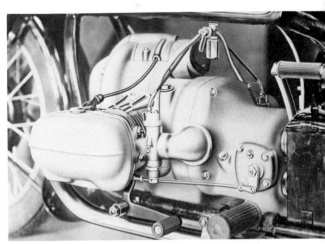

The completely new 500 cc flat-twin motor of the 1936 model R5 with the small air filters on the carburetors, affectionately known as ears, and the reversed foot-shifter with its adjustable linkage.

With the R5 BMW reintroduced the tubular frame, but it was a completely new design with arc-welded joints and oval-section tubes. All electrical components were now fully enclosed, and the toolbox ended up in the gas tank. Wheel rims began to sport their distinctive two-tone silver and black pattern, which reappeared again in the postwar 1951–54 models.

Riding a 1936 R5

Without a doubt the R5 is one of the great milestones in the history of BMW motorcycles—and it is easy to understand why. The 1936 model provided the basis for no less than twenty years of Munich flat twins. Intended as an option to the British single-cylinder models of the same capacity, the 500 cc BMW had to be on par both in performance and roadholding qualities. This was no mean achievement as the competition had been well established in the field of sporting models for quite some time. Gone was the typical BMW heaviness of the pressed-steel-framed 750 cc Boxers and the singles; the R5 fulfills its role as a high-performance model.

To tickle the floats before starting the engine one has to insert a finger in between the crankcase and the carburetors, as everything else is crammed in behind the huge cylinder heads. There is neither a choke lever for the carburetors nor a shutter on the small air filter, and only the ignition can be retarded with a small lever on the handlebar. The kick-start will be familiar to every Boxer owner; it is a side-swing unit that gives problems to most BMW novices, who often find it necessary to dismount from the machine in order to use it effectively.

With an impressive roar barely silenced by the fishtail mufflers, the engine comes to life, and after a little warming up the ticking valve noise from the alloy cylinder heads is no longer prominent. There is, however, quite a lot of mechanical clatter and whirr from different sources on the engine. The typical "clonk" accompanies the change from neutral into bottom gear by the inverted foot lever on the left-hand side of the gearbox, which works via an outside linkage. Letting in the clutch after having advanced the ignition, results in a rapid getaway with the slightest throttle opening.

The flat twin revs up with no bother and most of the mechanical noise gets drowned out by a mighty exhaust thunder. The way up through the four gears is easy and positive with the foot change. The acceleration feels brisk like you would expect from a sports model, and there is power right through the wide rev range, which climbs up to a high 5800 rpm. The official top speed of 87 mph should still be attainable without effort on a properly restored or well-maintained machine.

On the smooth road surfaces of today the comfortable ride of the R5 cannot really be judged against its girder-forked competitors from the 1930s. The oil-damped telescopic front forks can even be adjusted during the ride by interconnected levers on the fork top bolts. The difference in the damping action, however, is not readily felt; it may be of greater importance with a sidecar attached.

The rigid rear end of the frame is not so important, for the soft-sprung rubber saddle can keep up with changing road conditions. This also speaks volumes about the perfect design of the front forks that are responsible for the secure and effortless handling qualities of the R5 chassis. A well-arranged riding position with the tank firmly between the knees, a low saddle, almost flat handlebars and the footrests further back than on most other motorcycles—dictated by the wide cylinder spread—contributed to the favorable impression this fifty-four-year-old BMW gives even after a short test ride.

Seasoned members of the German BMW club tend to prefer the R5 to its plunger-framed successors for their long-distance rally events, saying that it handles better than the considerably heavier R51 models. It's definitely faster.

A central air filter housed in the gearbox marks this as the later 1937 R5. Most British journalists rated it as the perfect motorcycle, with a quality of ride, reliability, quietness and oil-tightness unheard of on contemporary British products.

With a new 600 side-valve engine in the R5 frame, the BMW R6 was intended as a modern touring mount or for sidecar use. Even though all BMW twins by this time had a foot-shifter, they all still retained a short hand-shift lever on the right side of the gearbox, which was actually a precise "neutral finder," and which was used quite often when coasting to a stop, thereby preventing needless, and potentially damaging, downshifts by means of the foot-shifter.

cover, the rather long timing chain also drove the generator, which was still mounted on top of the crankcase; the ignition coil and distributor were now mounted inside of the front cover. The clean and smooth surface of the new engine was enhanced by a new four-speed gearbox now operated through a linkage and an inverted foot lever on the left side. The transmission still retained a stubby additional hand lever on the right side.

A separate Amal carburetor was used on each cylinder head with neatly inward-turned small air filters, soon dubbed the ears by the motorcycling public. With 24 PS at 5800 rpm, the new BMW R5 showed that it had the potential to compete against the most powerful models of its class in the world. The top speed of about 87 mph was impressive but what really earned the R5

international praise was the handling qualities that made the power much more usable and led to impressive high average speeds. An attractive price below the R12 made the R5 the undisputed first choice for the sporting motorcyclist.

Compared to the narrow fenders without the familiar pinstriping seen on the R5, the R12 and R17 big twins were finished with pompous metalwork for 1937 resembling the flowing fenders of contemporary luxury cars. The only modification on the R5 in 1937 concerned the air intake, where a single wire-mesh air filter built into a cast extension of the gearbox casing was now connected via chrome tubes to the carburetors.

Following tradition, BMW introduced a new side-valve sibling to the R5, the 600 cc model R6 for 1937. Apart from the cylin-

Year and model	1936–1937 R5
Engine	Overhead-valve flat twin
Bore and stroke	68x68 mm
Displacement	494 cc
Horsepower	24 PS at 5800 rpm
Carburetion	Twin Amals, 22 mm
Ignition	Coil
Lubrication	Wet sump
Gearbox	Four-speed, foot actuated
Clutch	Single disc, dry
Frame	Twin tube
Suspension	Telescopic front forks; rigid rear
Brakes	Drum brakes front and rear
Wheels and tires	3.50x19 in.
Wheelbase	55 in.
Weight	364 lb.
Seat height	27 in.
Top speed	85 mph

One of the rarest of side-valve twins is this superbly restored 600 cc 1937 R6, which was the last of the tubular-frame "new generation" prewar twins to still have a rigid rear end. Its high torque and 18 PS made it a favorite among those who preferred sidecar touring. *Vintage BMW Bulletin, Larry Malinoski*

ders, the engine looked very similar to the R5 ohv unit, but now there was only one central camshaft used on the low-revving motor, which was driven by spur gears as in the early BMW engines.

The 18 PS R6 was clearly destined to replace the R12 as a long-lasting tourer, and more importantly, as a sidecar hauler. The German army authorities, however, were not interested, and in the middle of their

A plunger rear suspension transformed the R5 into the R51 in 1938. By now, stocks of chrome were being earmarked for gun barrels, so painted mufflers began to appear on all German machines.

The 750 cc side-valve engine 1938 R71 was the last of its kind. No more side-valve BMWs were built after World War II. During the war Harley- Davidson came out with its XA, which was a close copy of the shaft-drive R71.

enormous rearmament programs they preferred to stick to the trusted pressed-steel frame and its enduring qualities. Therefore the R12 was scheduled to remain in production in the single-carburetor 18 PS military version with magneto ignition and the orders for the R12 were further increased.

The civilian R12, even with its 20 PS from 750 cc, was completely outclassed by the R5, and was dropped along with the R17 from the BMW civilian program toward the end of 1937.

The new range had traditionally been unveiled at the Berlin Show and in February 1938 BMW made no exception. A plunger suspension for the rear wheel on the tubular frame had been anticipated as it had already been seen on the factory racers as well as on some of the team machines that were used in the International Six Days Trials in Wales in autumn 1937. Thus, in 1938 the R5 and R6 became the R51 and R61 with the new frame. In all there were four models shown with the modified frame as two new engines had been developed to cater to the discerning sidecar enthusiast. The R71 provided a

bored-out version of the side-valve engine with a cylinder bore of 78 instead of 70 mm. The new 750 cc motor gave 22 PS and an impressive torque range. It was quite easy to distinguish from the smaller version through the reintroduction of the old double-decker cylinder heads for better heat dissipation.

The second new model was presented as a sidecar sports machine with its 600 cc overhead-valve engine, but from the technical specification of the motor the true determination could be seen. It was not based on the R5/R51 unit with two camshafts and a long, whipping timing chain; instead it used the same crankcase as the side-valvers with one gear-driven camshaft in the center and a wide cylinder base incorporating the mounting for the pushrod tubes. This setup was preferred to the R5 design, which seemed to be more complicated than was really necessary. The power output of 30 PS at 5300 rpm was exceptional for a pushrod 600 cc and more than enough for towing a sidecar. The R66 therefore was destined as the top-of-the-range solo sports machine for the future, with a price considerably lower than the ear-

Year and model	1938–1941 R66
Engine	Overhead-valve flat twin
Bore and stroke	69.8x78 mm
Displacement	597 cc
Horsepower	30 PS at 5300 rpm
Carburetion	Twin Amals, 24 mm
Ignition	Coil
Lubrication	Wet sump
Gearbox	Four-speed, foot actuated
Clutch	Single disc, dry
Frame	Twin tube
Suspension	Telescopic front forks; plunger rear
Brakes	Drum brakes front and rear
Wheels and tires	3.50x19 in.
Wheelbase	55 in.
Weight	412 lb.
Seat height	28.3 in.
Top speed	90.5 mph

A bird's-eye view of the 1938 R71 reveals the narrow build of the tube-frame BMW; the flat cylinders were well out to the sides and received their share of cooling air. The Pagusa saddle logo and cable and control placement are clearly visible here, although the reason why the R71 is suspended from a rope is difficult to comprehend.

lier R17. The R66 weighed 412 lb. due to the additional bulk of the sprung frame, but the bike was still good for 95 mph.

Military R75

BMW was the biggest supplier of motorcycles to the German army when the Wehrmacht released their own specification for a special cross-country sidecar outfit to be used not only as a dispatch rider's vehicle but also as an attack vehicle for light motorized brigades to be set up as a modern cavalry. With a complete range of successful models in the summer of 1938, BMW was free to devote development time to the project as the commission was set as competition with Zündapp. One year later, the first prototypes were ready for evaluation by the army test department. The R71 engine was chosen although it tended to overheat during low speed off-road work and had to be supplanted by a better-suited design. There were other complaints as well, and the development program continued for another two years until production was started in June 1941.

The result was the BMW R75 and it would prove to be a great success as a total of nearly 18,000 units were built within less than three years. The 750 cc overhead-valve engine was built as a low-revving, high-torque motor, with all of the characteristics of the old side-valve sluggers. It gave 26 PS at 4000 rpm and was able to withstand a lot of abuse such as lugging along at walking pace in day-

long convoys. The valve covers were split into two separate pieces, held against the cylinder head by a claw anchored in the center. Under these covers, the rocker posts were no longer cast integrally with the main cylinder head casting but were bolted on separately. On top of the crankcase sat a new magneto from Noris with automatic ignition advance and the 6 volt generator, which was also from Noris rather than the traditional Bosch unit. The generator was bolted to the front engine cover, which housed timing and auxiliary drive gears that

The 600 cc overhead-valve engine of the 1938 R66 was not based on the R5 unit but on the

These massive rocker supports were part of the R66 cylinder head casting of 1938. Roller bearings for the rocker arms and hairpin valve springs were used. Lubricating oil for the valve gear was introduced via the knurled cap on the valve cover.

single-cam side-valver. The crankcase was therefore narrower than its predecessor.

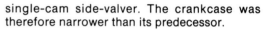

were helically cut. Two 24 mm carburetors from the Berlin firm Graetzin were modelled after the needle-jet-type Amal. The carburetors drew in their air from a cloth-element filter mounted on top of the gas tank, where the filter sat under a cover resembling a helmet.

The R75 gearbox had a four-speed cluster with the gears changed by a foot lever. In addition, there were two levers in a gate on the right-hand side of the gas tank: one of the levers engaged a different, higher ratio for off-road work; the other engaged the reverse gear. The driveshaft to the rear wheel drove a differential; power was taken from the differential to the bevel box at the rear wheel as well as to the sidecar wheel via a transverse shaft. The differential not only split the power between the two driven wheels in a ratio to suit the loads and the outfit's center of gravity to prevent the vehicle from running in circles, but the differential could also be locked to give full power on both rear wheels.

The frame of the R75 was a complete departure from the usual BMW design. A fabricated steel backbone held the steering

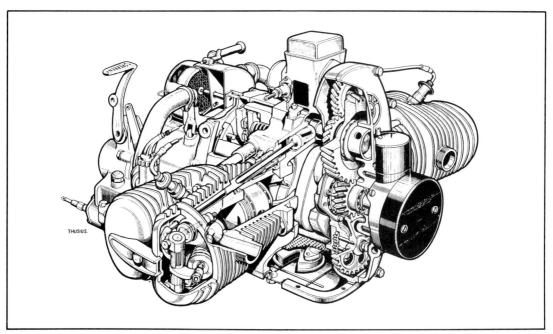

A sectioned view of an early R75 engine with the air filter still mounted on top of the gearbox. Under the black cover on the front end resides the generator. The lever on the gearbox is the rear-drive lock-out.

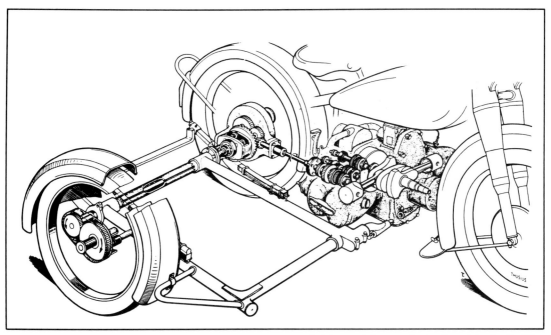

The drivetrain of the R75 included an additional high-ratio gearset and reverse on the gearbox, a limited-slip differential between the rear wheel and sidecar drive, and a lock-out for both. The sidecar chassis employed torsion-bar suspension.

The standard version of the R75 outfit as it was used by the German army during World War II with the air filter mounted on top of the gas tank, under what most Allied soldiers believed to be a spare steel helmet for the driver. The sidecar was by Steib. Almost everything seen in this photo is being reproduced today by enthusiasts in Germany, Italy and the United States, including replica MG34 machine guns! *Vintage BMW Bulletin, Rich Sheckler*

Early version of the R75 with the sidecar not fitted. Some models of the R75 were issued as solo machines, with the threaded connection for the sidecar drive blanked off with a large knurled cap. The misappellation R75m by which the R75 is often known stems from the fact that on the ID plate it reads *R75 m.Seitenwagen*, translated as R75 with sidecar. The correct name is simply R75.

Year and model	1938–1941 R71
Engine	Side-valve flat twin
Bore and stroke	78x78 mm
Displacement	745 cc
Horsepower	22 PS at 4600 rpm
Carburetion	Twin Graetzins, 24 mm
Ignition	Coil
Lubrication	Wet sump
Gearbox	Four-speed, hand actuated
Clutch	Single disc, dry
Frame	Twin tube
Suspension	Telescopic front forks; plunger rear
Brakes	Drum brakes front and rear
Wheels and tires	3.50x19 in.
Wheelbase	55 in.
Weight	412 lb.
Seat height	28.3 in.
Top speed	78 mph

Year and model	1941–1944 R75
Engine	Overhead-valve flat twin
Bore and stroke	78x78 mm
Displacement	745 cc
Horsepower	26 PS at 4000 rpm
Carburetion	Twin Graetzins, 24 mm
Ignition	Noris magneto
Lubrication	Wet sump
Gearbox	Four-speed, foot actuated, hand change for reverse and high-ratio gears
Clutch	Single disc, dry
Frame	Bolt-up tubes
Suspension	Telescopic front forks; rigid rear
Brakes	Drum brakes front and rear, the latter with hydraulic operation
Wheels and tires	5.00x16 in.
Wheelbase	56.8 in.
Weight	620 lb. without sidecar
Seat height	28.3 in.
Top speed	58 mph

head stock which was welded on and all the other parts of the duplex frame were suspended from that center piece. Lengths of tube were butted at the ends and bolted together. A steel pressing strengthened the rear frame between the end of the central section and the bottom tubes. The upper part of the engine was also strutted to that point under the saddle. The 16 in. wheels were shod with substantial 4.50 section knobby tires and large 250 mm drum brakes on all three wheels had to cope with stopping this outfit, which had a dry weight of 925 lb. The rear and the sidecar brakes were hydraulic.

In the hands of an experienced rider the BMW R75 and its counterpart from Zündapp, the KS 750, were no match for any other vehicle even under the most appalling conditions, but they were expensive to produce and finally gave way to the mass-produced German Jeep-type car from Volkswagen.

Prospects

Most BMWs from the 1930s have seen a long active life, especially the R5 and R51, as they were still competitive in the marketplace and on the racetracks twenty years later. Restoring the 1930s BMWs to original specification became popular from the early 1970s on when they finally were acknowledged as collector's vehicles. It is still not difficult in Germany to find quite a good

selection of spare parts, either in used condition or remanufactured through the BMW Veteran Club's efforts. But the acquisition of a good original model can pose problems.

The most widely available is the R12 with a total production of 36,000, many having been in military service throughout Europe. It is not difficult to give an R12 a good civilian paint job in black with white pinstriping, but almost all of the machines coming from Greece or Poland are so worn out that any mechanical refurbishment is going to need to be comprehensive and thus costly.

The overhead-valve R5 and R51 have become popular for vintage racing, to the point, in fact, where several sidecar outfits have been seen so heavily modified that the only thing that seems to make them eligible for the prewar class is the distinctive valve covers. Nevertheless, the sporting BMWs of the 1930s are a good choice for all sorts of use, be it an old bike rally or long-distance motorcycle touring. One can easily see why they were called the most modern motorcycles of their day.

Judging from the number coming onto the German market, BMW's last side-valve R71 must have survived in large numbers. There is an interesting reason for this. In addition to the 3,458 units made by BMW at the Munich factory between 1938 and 1941, there was a copy called the M-72 which was built under license starting in 1939 in Moscow. This was turned out in large numbers for a long time in unchanged form with the 750 cc side-valve engine surviving in an updated chassis until recently. It obviously seemed to be a good idea to some people to restore a Russian M–72 to BMW R71 specifications, and with remanufactured parts like the tank badges or the identification plate that is riveted to the steering head, all Russian origins can be hidden. Any knowledgeable BMW enthusiast can spot the difference by the quality of the castings, welds and other things such as the lack of German Fischer-Amal carburetors, but a newcomer still can be fooled by the Russian BMW lookalike.

The most expensive project will turn out to be the R75, which is also quite common on the market. There has been a steady demand from all over the world for quite a while, but more R75s still turn up every day as they now command very high prices. The complex drivetrain may not always have been serviced and rebuilt properly when no spares were at hand, but some experienced specialists are always able to help, and more replacement parts are once again being made.

Ratings

There are clear favorites within the 1930s range, even more than amongst the early models. Attracting not only the BMW en-thusiast but collectors of military vehicles as well as somebody who is interested in the outstanding capabilities of the sidecar outfit, the R75 is a clear five-star model. This is also significantly reflected in the prices asked for them.

First choice for the solo rider would be the sporting R5 or the plunger-frame R66 with the more powerful 600 cc engine. Still rarer than the latter is the R17, which looks like a behemoth but is nevertheless a fast mount with quite a pedigree, and only 434 were ever made. Five stars to all of them.

Close behind is the four-star rating for the leaf-spring R16 and the plunger-rear-end R51. Even in Germany the remaining models must be rated four stars. The side-valve R11, R12, R6, R61 and R71 are not quite as popular as the more sporting ohv models, but they are becoming too rare to be ranked at three stars any longer. Outside their Fatherland, and especially in the United States, the situation is clear. Nobody seriously interested in buying a BMW of the 1930s would turn down an R12, even a well-restored civilized ex-Wehrmacht model. Today, even former military machines can be included in that category, as there seems to be an amazingly large demand for them, and well-executed detail work is always appreciated.

Chapter 3

Flat Twins
1950–1969

Model	Years	Type	Rating
R51/2	1950–1951	500 cc ohv	★★★★
R51/3	1951–1954	500 cc ohv	★★★★
R67	1951	600 cc ohv	★★★★
R67/2	1952–1954	600 cc ohv	★★★★
R68	1952–1954	600 cc ohv	★★★★★
R50	1955–1960	500 cc ohv	★★★★
R69	1955–1960	600 cc ohv	★★★★
R67/3	1955–1956	600 cc ohv	★★★★
R60	1956–1960	600 cc ohv	★★★★
R50/2	1960–1969	500 cc ohv	★★★★
R60/2	1960–1969	600 cc ohv	★★★★
R50S	1960–1962	500 cc ohv	★★★★
R69S	1960–1969	600 cc ohv	★★★★
R50US	1967–1969	500 cc ohv	★★★★
R60US	1967–1969	600 cc ohv	★★★★
R69US	1967–1969	600 cc ohv	★★★★

After the end of World War II the future for BMW seemed to be in doubt. As a major contributor to the German war effort, the Munich aircraft engine plant was subjected to heavy bombing, and what was left had to be dismantled as reparations to the victors. Motorcycle production had been transferred to the Eisenach car plant in 1942, and this factory was now situated in the Russian zone. After some kitchen and bakery equipment—including alloy pots made from melted-down cylinder head castings—had been produced, a group of engineers was formed to prepare drawings and tooling for future motorcycle production. Things were in such devastation that the engineers had to start by taking a prewar model apart to get measurements, since all drawings had been lost.

In December 1948 production was started again with the R24 single, which was soon in demand worldwide. In the first year, no less than 9,400 motorcycles left the rebuilt factory in Munich and a new flat-twin model was promised to follow.

The R51/2 twin was first shown on the cover of the German magazine *Das Motorrad* just before Christmas 1949, but buyers had to wait for some months before the first 1,000 units were constructed, which were in turn painted in dark grey and earmarked for the French police forces. During the 1950 season the R51/2 finally became available to private customers both in Germany and abroad, and as the designation implied, it was based on the old prewar R51.

The most significant differences between the prewar and postwar motorcycles were the new split valve covers on the cylinder heads, which were similar to those of the R75. Other changes had been made underneath the heads as well. Inclined carburetors from Bing and a valanced front fender were also new. The handlebars on the R51/2 were changed from 1 to ⅞ in. diameter, and featured normally pivoted control levers versus the older inverted-pivot levers. The gearbox gained a coil spring damper on the mainshaft and the telescopic front forks two-way damping via a new valve design.

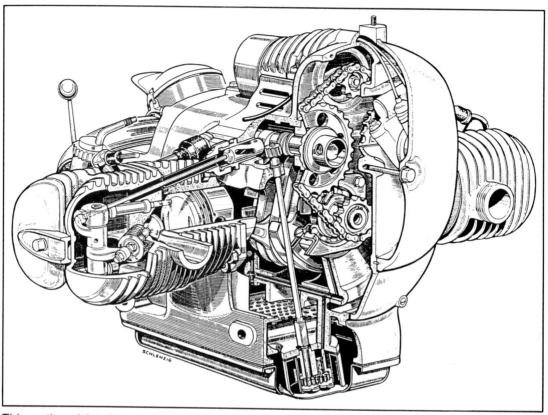

This sectioned drawing reveals the chain-driven two-camshaft setup that was the same on the 1950 R51/2 as on the R5. New cylinder heads and coil-type valve springs are used here as well as a scooped cover over the wire-mesh air filter.

New also were two strengthening tubes on the frame, one of them in front of the rear fender between two short cross tubes, welded in between the top and bottom twin tubes. The other was a T-shaped piece cross-bracing the twin downtubes at the front and running backwards under the tank to the joint of the single top tube with the rear tubes. The mounting of the adjustable saddle (adjustable for height and support) remained unchanged, but the Bosch taillamp was a new pattern, while the headlamp remained virtually the same as before. One thing was noted only after close inspection; the pattern of the pinstripes had been changed with the thin line now inside the wider one, not the other way round as it had been before.

With the R51/2 BMW regained a prominent position in the international motorcycle market, but an updated prewar design was not enough, even if the R51 had been years ahead of its time. The BMW development team regarded the R51/2 as only a temporary solution while they concentrated on a new 500 cc engine. When the new ohv twin made its first public appearance at the Amsterdam Motor Show in February 1951, the bike was not that much different in looks, and the new model designation, R51/3, was no great help either. Contrary to popular conception, however, there was a completely new engine in the old frame and not just another update. Ribbed one-piece valve covers on the engine and new pinstriping on the front fender that no longer followed the

Year and model	1951–1954 R51/3
Engine	Overhead-valve flat twin
Bore and stroke	68x68 mm
Displacement	494 cc
Horsepower	24 PS at 5800 rpm
Carburetion	Twin Bings, 22 mm
Ignition	Noris magneto
Lubrication	Wet sump
Gearbox	Four-speed
Clutch	Single disc, dry
Frame	Twin tube
Suspension	Telescopic front forks; plunger rear
Brakes	Drum brakes front and rear, twin-leading shoe front from 1952 on
Wheels and tires	3.50x19 in.
Wheelbase	55 in.
Weight	419 lb.
Seat height	28.3 in.
Top speed	87 mph

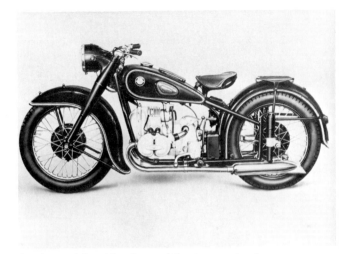

A valanced front fender and the two-part valve covers distinguish this 1950 R51/2 from the pre-war R51.

edge but drew in the shape of a narrow sports fender, and the front brace mounted over the front fender top, were the only obvious differences between the R51/2 and the R51/3.

The R51/3 bore and stroke dimensions remained at a square 68x68 mm as well as the power output of 24 PS at 5800 rpm, but internally quite a lot had been redesigned. A single camshaft driven by helical-cut gears replaced the twin-cam design with the long timing chain that had always been prone to undue whipping and susceptible to wear. The new crankcase was much narrower but the front cover bulged still more, as it now housed a generator driven from the front end of the crankshaft and a contact breaker set with the auto advance mechanism attached to the camshaft. A third spur gear was situated below the main drive gear from the crankshaft driving the oil pump behind it. The oil pump was no longer situated on the bottom of the crankcase where it had formerly been operated by a long quill shaft from the camshaft. New pistons with four rings were introduced, and the valve clearances could now be adjusted at the pushrod

The last twin-camshaft pushrod production BMW was this 1950 R51/2, lovingly restored here by a United States Vintage Club member from Ohio. The finned housing on the top is nothing more than a functional cooling clamp for the generator, which was driven by the same chain that spun the two camshafts. *Vintage BMW Bulletin, Bill Kuhlman*

Also new in 1950 were the inclined Bing carburetors on the 500 cc flat twin R51/2.

The typical German sprung Pagusa saddle with its strong central coil spring, seen here on a 1950 R51/2. This was also the last BMW to have an external wiring harness clipped to the outside of the rear fender.

ends of the rockers. The small engine plate on top of the crankcase no longer simply anchored the timing case to the twin down-tubes but now connected the top housing to the strengthening tube under the tank.

A new style of air filter was mounted into the casing on top of the gearbox and consisted of a replaceable paper element under a black tin cover held on by a central bolt. Inside the gearbox the only novelty was an electric contact for a neutral gear warning light set into the headlamp. The front brake was beefed up by narrow strengthening ribs cast onto the iron brake drum to prevent distortion under too much heat. Without changing the shape visibly, the gas tank now held 17 liters or 4½ gallons instead of 14 liters or 3½ gallons, and was fitted with thinner knee grips.

As the third generation of the R51 series, the R51/3 was not the only new model available after the spring of 1951. With different dimensions for bore and stroke of 72x73 mm, an additional 600 cc version was offered

The R51/3 from 1951 used a new single-cam-shaft engine in the old frame. It is easily recognizable by the new cylinder head covers and redesigned engine cases and covers, now housing a magneto and a generator, all safe, warm and dry.

alongside the 500. The R67 was not the expected successor to the well-remembered and powerful R66. With only 26 PS, it lacked the thinly disguised sporting character of the prewar model and was intended purely as a sidecar machine. The power output, however, was soon increased to 28 PS for the second production year and now called the R67/2. The otherwise unchanged R67/2 was on par with the Zündapp KS 601, its rival flat-twin from Nuremberg.

With a comparatively high production run of more than 6,000 Boxers annually, a lot of small detail modifications were introduced without prior announcement to the public and only the authorized dealers were notified through the official service notes sent from the factory on a regular basis. There were, for example, two instead of three bronze bushes as rocker bearings after the first 2,000 engines had been produced, and a second oil scraping piston ring was added towards the bottom of the skirt soon after that. More distinct changes that were easy to recognize could be found in the brochures for the 1952 models. There was a new cover over yet another style of air filter, which enclosed the filter much better and was painted silver. The new filter also had a lever to choke the intake air for cold starts. The front brake was changed to a twin-leading-shoe model which acted without a fixed linkage, but by contracting the two levers between the inner wire and the outer conduit

Year and model	1952–1954 R67/2
Engine	Overhead-valve flat twin
Bore and stroke	72x73 mm
Displacement	594 cc
Horsepower	28 PS at 5600 rpm
Carburetion	Twin Bings, 24 mm
Ignition	Noris magneto
Lubrication	Wet sump
Gearbox	Four-speed
Clutch	Single disc, dry
Frame	Twin tube
Suspension	Telescopic front forks; plunger rear
Brakes	Drum brakes, twin-leading shoe at the front
Wheels and tires	3.50x19 in.
Wheelbase	55 in.
Weight	423 lb.
Seat height	28.3 in.
Top speed	90 mph

In 1954 the R51/3 and its 600 cc sibling, the R67/2, were updated with full-width duplex hubs, alloy rims, new mufflers and a fully covered air filter.

of the brake cable. Also new for the 1952 season were rubber gaiters on the front forks instead of the prewar-style steel covers over the stanchions.

In Germany the R51/3 held a unique position as being the only 500 cc motorcycle in production and there was little competition from imported models. But the situation was different on the important export markets where the British parallel twins were far ahead in both performance and price. Since there were even more powerful 650 cc versions coming from Triumph and BSA, the BMW could no longer be offered just as a sporting mount, and a rumored high-performance model was eagerly awaited from Munich.

In October 1951, a new model was displayed at the Frankfurt Motor Cycle Show looking much like the International Six Days Trial machines of the factory team. This was the new flagship of the range and it was nothing less than the expected 100 mph roadburner. The R68 boasted a redesigned 600 cc engine that delivered 35 PS at 7000 rpm, and the high-level two-into-one exhaust system on the right-hand side was

only intended as a sort of styling exercise to give the new model a different appearance. When the new R68 finally was available during summer 1952, it wore standard low-level fishtail exhausts.

The sporting performance was underlined by the equipment, as the R68 was furnished with a narrow front fender, making a more substantial tubular fork brace necessary, and there was a special pillion pad fitted to the rear fender and attached to the saddle to swing up and down with it. A pair of non-folding additional footrests were not only there for the occasional passenger on the pillion seat, but they also allowed the rider to try a more racey feet-to-the-rear position.

New valve covers gave a hint of the different engine specification, as the twin-rib design resembled the older pattern but all in a one-piece casting. Underneath the covers were bigger valves with an inlet of 38 mm and an exhaust of 34 mm instead of the former 34 and 32 mm, respectively. The new rockers worked on needle bearings. The compression ratio was increased from 5.6:1 to 7.5:1, and together with a new camshaft and 26 mm Bing carburetors (versus 22 mm

BMW MOTORCYCLES

150-16 14th AVE., WHITESTONE, NEW YORK • FLUSHING 3-0053

1951 BMW PRICE LIST:

PRICES SHOWN ARE F.O.B. NEW YORK

SPECIFICATIONS AND PRICES ARE SUBJECT TO CHANGE

MODEL	LIST PRICE	EXCISE TAX	RETAIL PRICE
R 51-2, Battery Ignition, Front & Rear Springing, Shaft Drive, 500 cc Twin, 24 HP, Top Speed 90 MPH	$ 975.00	$ 52.00	$1,027.00
R 51-3, Magneto Ignition, Front & Rear Springing, Shaft Drive, 500 cc Twin, 24 HP, Top Speed 95 MPH	$1,027.00	$ 53.00	$1,080.00
R-67, Magneto Ignition, Front & Rear Springing, Shaft Drive, 600 cc Twin, 26 HP, Top Speed 100 MPH	$1,070.00	$ 56.00	$1,126.00
R-25, Battery Ignition, Front & Rear Springing, Shaft Drive, 250 cc Single, 12 HP, Top Speed 80 MPH	$ 639.00	$ 33.00	$ 672.00
Side-Car, "Special" to fit above models, with spare Wheel & Tire, Luggage Rack, Windshield & Cover.	$ 376.00	$ 20.00	$ 396.00

An original 1951 price list from the US importer of BMW motorcycles. Amazingly, fairly complete and even mechanically sound and running BMWs can still be found today at asking prices similar to the prices in this ad of 40 years ago! Sidecars, on the other hand, have increased in price nearly tenfold. *Vintage BMW Bulletin, Richard Kahn*

Year and model	1952-1954 R68
Engine	Overhead-valve flat twin
Bore and stroke	72x73 mm
Displacement	594 cc
Horsepower	35 PS at 7000 rpm
Carburetion	Twin Bings, 26 mm
Ignition	Noris magneto
Lubrication	Wet sump
Gearbox	Four-speed
Clutch	Single disc, dry
Frame	Twin tube
Suspension	Telescopic front forks; plunger rear
Brakes	Drum brakes, twin-leading shoe front
Wheels and tires	3.50x19 in.
Wheelbase	55 in.
Weight	425 lb.
Seat height	28.5 in.
Top speed	100 mph

on the R51/3 and 24 mm on the R67/2), the R68 engine delivered 35 PS at 7000 rpm. In an effort to keep the flexing of the crankshaft under control at high rpm, a special type of main bearing was used on the rear end with slightly barrel-shaped rollers.

Further modifications led to the updated appearance of the 1953 models with full-width hubs, straight-pull spokes and alloy wheel rims replacing the painted steel ones, which were formerly black with a silver center band. New cigar-shaped mufflers with tubular rear ends replaced the fishtails.

Unfortunately for the export market this was not enough, as the plunger frame was getting a bit long in the tooth, having been around since 1938. It was obviously more of a disadvantage for a sports machine like the R68 if the performance of the engine was to

Perhaps the most famous, original, unrestored postwar BMW twin in the United States is this 1953 R67/2, which was the first BMW sold through a dealer, Freeman's Cycle, Hamilton, Massachusetts. It remained with the original owner Lou Rizoli for 20 years, and is now with its fourth owner, resting happily in warm and sunny California. *Vintage BMW Bulletin, Marie Lacko*

The R67/3 was furnished with steel rims and an 18 in. rear wheel as a sidecar hauler. It is shown with the Steib TR500, sold as the BMW Spezial sidecar, which was installed at the BMW factory prior to delivery.

be fully utilized. The short travel of the rear wheel springing set a natural limit on inferior road surfaces. A rear swing-arm suspension was expected as this was one of the most expensive motorcycles on the market outside Germany, but unlike the racing machines, the road models did not receive a redesigned rear end in 1954.

It was not as simple as just grafting a swing-arm design to the existing frame, however. Some specials builders had done it in their workshops, but the development engineers at BMW had to come up with an original solution in the old tradition of the Munich firm's policy of achieving new levels of design and quality. The long wait came to an end in January 1955 when two new BMW motorcycles were the main attraction of the Brussels Motor Show. And a big surprise

they were from stem to stern, for not only did the rear wheel get a swing-arm suspension, but the front wheel as well! First developed by Englishman Ernie Earles some years before, the leading-link Earles fork setup was perfected by BMW in several ways. The main tubes were angled back from the level of the steering head bottom to behind the front wheel where the fork that held the wheel was held on a fixed axle. Just behind the wheel axle the suspension struts with hydraulic dampers and coiled springs covered under shrouds were bolted to the fork tubes connecting them to the main tubes. The cross-bracing tube above the fork axle between the main tubes and the bottom fork crown were substantial parts, whereas the top crown was only a steel plate. The front brake was anchored to the right swing arm and the fender was held by bolts at the center tube of the fork and by the U-stay over its front end. Taper roller bearings were not only found in the wheel hubs but also on the fork pivots and rear swing-arm connections.

Remaining familiar only in its center section, the frame still had its single top and twin downtube setup with a strengthening

A twin-leading-shoe front brake was introduced to the Boxer range in 1952. The narrow fender identifies this model as 1953 R68.

Another R51/3, this time a 1952 model, still with the characteristic metal fork covers, which were finally replaced with rubber gaiters on all twins in 1953. The finned exhaust nuts are accessory items which fitted over the plated-steel ring clamps. *Vintage BMW Bulletin, Tracy Baker*

tube running under the tank from the front to the seat mount. The rear part now consisted of two complete loops that were welded to the bottom tubes under the gearbox, which curved up on both sides of the rear wheel and met at the rear end of the top tube where they were welded on. On top of the curved section on each side, a substantial steel cup was welded via a short outrigger profile and similar suspension units to those on the front end were mounted into the attachments. Into each loop a slightly curved tube was set to hold the rear swing arm and two smaller tubes cross-braced the setup. While the left half of the link was the usual small-diameter tube, the other half had to be a much bigger affair as the driveshaft ran inside it. The bevel box with crown wheel and pinion was bolted directly to the end of that housing and was connected with the

suspension strut. Because a swing-arm axle running across the frame could not be used with a driveshaft running inside one fork leg, screwed-in pivot pins held the rear swing arm into the frame, again pivoting on tapered roller bearings. The suspension springs could be adjusted for the load of a passenger by a short lever at the bottom without need of special tools.

Using the same engines as before, the 500 cc model was now called the R50 and the larger capacity sports model was termed the R69. Alongside both, the sidecar hauler remained available with the old plunger frame, but the model code R67/3 denoted some modifications. Plain-bearing big ends were developed but not put in production as they were only reliable in the heavily loaded and low-revving sidecar outfits of the German highway rescue patrol. So the R67/3 was only produced with higher sidecar gearing, chrome-plated steel wheel rims and a fatter 4.00x19 in. rear tire as standard. The new swing-arm chassis of the R50 and R69 rolled on 18 in. wheels front and rear, and

The high-performance 1954 600 cc R68 is immediately recognized by its new cylinder heads and valve covers, finned exhaust clamps, sprung pillion seat connected to the rider's saddle, and chrome lifting handle on the rear fender instead of a pressed-steel parcel rack. The narrow sports front fender was also only used on the R68.

State of the art in 1954, a 600 cc R68 could probably keep up with this DC-3—at least on the runway. The 1954 R68 differed from earlier R68s by having more powerful, larger brakes in cast-alloy drums, and by having alloy rims and the new style larger headlamp with covered key slide.

was laid out perfectly for attaching a sidecar, with the leading-link front end being far better suited to a sidecar outfit than the telescopic forks with their tendency to twist under heavy side loadings. Obviously the R67/3 was aimed as a budget motorcycle for fleet buyers from police forces or the like.

Year and model	1955-69 R50
Engine	Overhead-valve flat twin
Bore and stroke	68x68 mm
Displacement	494 cc
Horsepower	26 PS at 5800 rpm
Carburetion	Twin Bings, 24 mm
Ignition	Noris magneto
Lubrication	Wet sump
Gearbox	Four-speed
Clutch	Single disc, dry
Frame	Twin tube
Suspension	Swing arm front and rear
Brakes	Drums, twin-leading shoe at the front
Wheels and tires	3.50x18 in.
Wheelbase	55.7 in.
Weight	430 lb.
Seat height	28.5 in.
Top speed	87 mph

All new, however, was the gearbox on the Earles-forked models with its three-shaft layout made necessary by an improved shock-absorbing system on the input shaft. Also changed was the operating of the single-disc dry clutch. Built into the flywheel as before, it now worked with a diaphragm center spring.

With the new rear wheel springing and its longer travel, the shaft-drive had to be redesigned. On the R67/3 and all earlier plunger-frame models, a round coupling made from hard rubber had been enough to compensate for the limited longitudinal movement of the shaft where it was connected to the gearbox. The limited suspension travel was taken up by the universal joint between the drive-shaft and the rear-wheel drive pinion. Now, with the R50 and R69 the universal joint was moved to the gearbox side and changes in shaft length during suspension travel were compensated for by a splined yoke at the other end.

A slight increase in the compression ratio, and the 24 mm carburetors from the R67, gave 26 instead of 24 PS for the 500 cc engine, which enabled the R50 to reach 90 mph. While the top speed of the R69 remained on a par with the best roadburners at 102 mph, the manners of this top-of-the-line BMW had changed completely from the earlier R68. It was now regarded as the most civilized high-speed machine of its day, which made lengthy cruising at 90 mph on Autobahn or motorway effortless for both the engine and the rider.

A third model, the R60, that was positioned between the R50 and R69, became available from 1956 on. The R60 was nothing less than the 28 PS 600 cc engine from R67 in the new swing-arm chassis. It was primarily offered as the new sidecar machine to replace the R67/3. Still, the Earles forks were adaptable for sidecars on the other models as well; by simply slotting the pivot pin of the front swing arm into the alternative forward position to shorten the front wheel's trail and to provide less steering effort with a sidecar attached to the frame.

Meanwhile the situation affecting the German motorcycle market had changed dramatically. The year 1957 not only saw the

Occasionally one gets lucky! This 600 cc R68, one of the most desirable of the 1950–69 era BMWs, was found in this condition in New Jersey in 1984. Correct for this 1953 R68 are the non-finned mufflers and the small, twin-lens taillamp. All that's missing is the chrome grab handle which would fit the two holes on top of the fender. *Vintage BMW Bulletin, Marie Lacko*

Year and model	1960–1969 R69S
Engine	Overhead-valve flat twin
Bore and stroke	72x73 mm
Displacement	594 cc
Horsepower	42 PS at 7000 rpm
Carburetion	Twin Bings, 26 mm
Ignition	Bosch magneto
Gearbox	Four-speed
Clutch	Single disc, dry
Frame	Twin tube
Suspension	Swing arm front and rear
Brakes	Drums, twin-leading shoe at the front
Wheels and tires	3.50x18 in.
Wheelbase	55.7 in.
Weight	445 lb.
Seat height	28.5 in.
Top speed	109 mph

With the R51/3 engine, swing-arm frame, Earles front forks and reshaped gas tank, the R50 went into production in 1955. This is a first-year model.

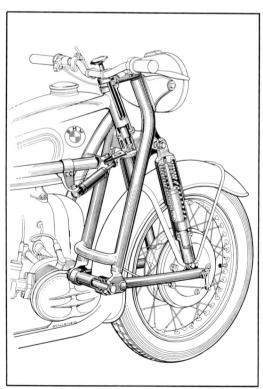

The leading-link Earles-type front forks, seen here with the hydraulic steering damper of the R50S and R69S.

end for famous makes like Adler, DKW and Horex, but also a drastic cut in production at BMW. A new record output of 29,699 motorcycles had been reached only three years before, but now the Munich factory was down to less than 5,500 units with remaining stock from 1955 and 1956 still unsold at the dealers as well as at the factory. A somewhat better picture was seen via increased response from foreign markets, especially in the United States, where demand for the Munich Boxers was steadily increasing. With 85 percent of the flat twins going abroad, production had to be increased again and further development efforts seemed possible.

At the same time, the BMW car division was in serious trouble. The big V–8-powered limousines never earned the factory enough profit, while the small bubble car Isetta was just not the right thing to lead BMW back to success. The financial situation became worse by the end of 1959 and a takeover by Mercedes-Benz seemed to be the best solution, but at the last minute this was postponed and the sporty BMW 700 car with a motorcycle-derived flat-twin engine at the rear turned things in the right direction. BMW cars went from strength to

The R68 engine was used for the new R69. An early 1955 model is pictured here, which still had the small rear light, although the larger "coffee can" taillamps were available as accessory items.

strength from then on and it was with a new atmosphere of optimism that the latest BMW motorcycles were shown to the press in August 1960 on the famous Nurburgring race circuit.

Since the last new item on the BMWs had been a bigger taillamp lamp in 1957, quite a lot of detail work had gone into the engines to extract more power and to increase their reliability. Beefed-up crankshafts and camshafts, strengthened bearing housings in the crankcase, hard-chromed piston rings, improved ventilation from crankcase and gearbox, new cam followers and a stronger clutch assembly were the main changes found on all flat-twin engines. The 500 cc model was now called the R50/2 with no external differences from its R50 forerunner, but the R60/2 now produced 30 PS based on a higher compression ratio of 7.5:1 instead of 6.5:1.

The R69 was replaced by two new models with more powerful engines. The same 35 PS was now available from a 500 cc engine in

While this 1959 R69, complete with period Aero windshield and headlight guard, might not have pleased your local Harley-Davidson riders, the young lady and her kidney belt would surely have caught their eye! Only the sharp-eyed enthusiast, however, would know that this is an R69 and not the later R69S, for only the R69 had a handlebar-mounted manual spark control lever, clearly visible in the photo. *Vintage BMW Bulletin, Zintgrafp Photos*

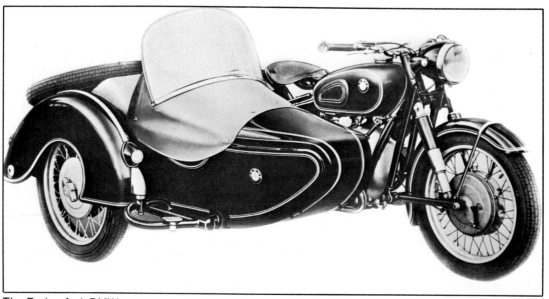

The Earles-fork BMW was considered to be the ultimate sidecar machine. This is a 1960 R60, fitted with the BMW Spezial version of the Steib TR500.

Rear-wheel bevel drive box and extra-strong mounting of the hand-adjustable suspension units on the Earles-fork R50, R60 and R69 BMWs.

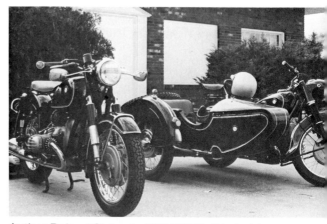

Author Roland Slabon's 1966 R50/2, fitted with VDO tachometer, Hagus headlamp mirrors, flat fender rack and bar-end signals of the era. Note that the camshaft-driven tachometer requires relocation of the Klaxon horn to the right side of the engine. Next to the R50/2 is its stablemate, an all-original, unrestored 1954 R67/2 and Spezial sidecar, as delivered by the factory, in black rather than the customary forest green, to the Rosenheim, Bavaria, Verkehrspolizei on October 22, 1954. *Vintage BMW Bulletin, Marie Lacko*

the new R50S, even though at a very high level 7650 rpm, which would impact reliability. At lower revs but at a higher compression ratio of 9.5:1, the reworked 600 cc sports engine gave 42 PS at 7000 rpm in the R69S. Both engines had the familiar cylinder heads with rockers on needle bearings and the two rib covers, but on the R50S only the valve stems were larger, while the valve heads remained the same size as on the R50. The inlet ports were enlarged, however, and 26 mm Bing carburetors were now fitted. Larger air filter assemblies and mufflers also contributed to better gas-air flow on both engines. A closer spread between the gear ratios in the four-speed gearboxes and a hydraulic steering damper activated by the knob on the steering head via a short link were other novelties. First seen only on the German home-market models, Hella indicator lights were fitted to the ends of the handlebars, but these could be purchased at the accessory counter for the export models as well.

While it seemed that the flat-twin BMWs had reached a level of perfection that would

A late 1960s publicity shot for some of the latest New York fashions. This R50/2 twin has the distinctive US market high handlebars, the standard 4 gallon gas tank with the toolbox on the left-hand side and chrome wheel rims. *Vintage BMW Bulletin, Richard Kahn*

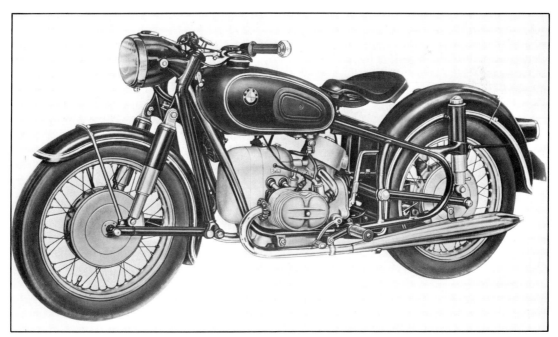

This 1960 R50S of 35 PS can only be distinguished through its smaller cylinder heads from the 600 cc R69S model. This example is equipped with Hella bar-end turn signals.

This is the typical BMW of the 1960s, the R69S
sports model with the dual seat as most commonly sold in the United States.

The R69S engine can be recognized by the anti-
vibration damper disc on the front end of the
crankshaft, which was introduced in September
1963.

It seems everyone got into the spirit of things back in the 1960s, including a Miss America hopeful! This R69S carries a small fortune in period accessories: an Avon Avonaire fairing, teardrop Enduro saddlebags, extra-large Heinrich gas tank, leather hand warmers and a matched pair of Albert handlebar mirrors. *Vintage BMW Bulletin, Bill Wilson Studio*

Another prizewinner at a US Vintage Club meet: John Delorenzo's 1963 R69S, shown here with the correct accessories of the period, such as the large 6 gallon gas tank, leather tank cover, bar-end signals, folding Denfeld luggage rack and extra-wide dual seat, all popular US accessories. The use of the factory one-piece crash-bar required the relocation of the horn to the left side of the engine. *Vintage BMW Bulletin, Marie Lacko*

assure healthy sales for quite some time, this was true only on foreign markets because there were a few problems with the S models in Germany. Nowhere else were they ridden as hard and fast as on the German Autobahn, and street races with owners of powerful British vertical twins could lead to reliability troubles. While the British bikes were not well-suited to long-distance Autobahn runs, they showed quicker handling on winding roads, which meant a lot of revs and gear changing for the BMW riders if they wanted to keep up. High revs were BMW's problem on the Autobahn, as well. BMW would not have been BMW if their's was not a quick response to reported engine failures. The first improvements were more substantial bottom flanges on the cylinder barrels from April 1962 on, and later in the same year the peaky and overstressed R50S was

dropped from the program. Nevertheless, the R50S motor saw more use in 500 cc class racing, whereas the larger-capacity R69S was preferred on the road. In September 1963 a little flywheel-like vibration damper was mounted to the crankshaft in front of the generator to dampen the flexing of the shaft at top revs, and from then on the R69S behaved as expected.

Many small modifications added year after year were all part of the Munich company's philosophy that improving the quality of their products should never stop. But as successful as they were with their clientele, made up mostly of a small, dedicated group of motorcyclists, discerning long-distance tourers or sporting mounts for well-heeled gentleman racers to keep pace with the motorcycle boom of the 1960s was not in the cards for BMW. Where only raw engine power and fashionable looks counted, the British twins were the force to reckon with, whereas the BMWs were considered at best conservative models from a past period, well

From 1967 on, completely new long-travel telescopic front forks—the forerunner of the /5 telescopic forks—were optional equipment for the US market. Sidecar lugs on the right-hand side of the frame were also deleted, although some US-fork equipped models did arrive with the older frames. This is an R69US.

manufactured and long lasting but not too exciting. At the same time when small gas tanks, slim seats, lots of chrome plating and flashy colors were the order of the day, BMW still had a large 24 liter or 6¼ gallon as well as a standard 17 liter or 4½ gallon gas tank, a huge dual seat, and white as the only optional color over the deep glossy black.

The only attempt at modernization was the new long-travel telescopic front forks that became available only on special order during 1967 for the US market. The forks were said to improve the off-road capabilities of the machine, but as the factory trials riders had used the Earles forks on their mounts before, the move could only be regarded as an attempt to gain lost territory in the US sales figures where the old Earles-fork setup really did look antiquated.

The telescopic-fork models were termed the R50US, R60US and the R69US. If BMW wanted to participate in the prospering new motorcycle market, which had turned completely from everyday and ride-to-work vehicles to highly sophisticated sports and pastime instruments, they had to come up with some new ideas. Against the background of a successful automobile division in Munich, there was no doubt that a modern BMW for the 1970s would soon have to be released.

Prospects

With 31,276 plunger-framed Boxers and nearly 70,000 Earles-fork twins produced between 1950 and 1969 there are still quite a number of them around. With large export sales, especially of the latter models, many are still in good supply outside of Germany.

As the traditional BMW motorcycles, they have become more and more attractive to collectors in recent years, but there have always been more people interested in re-building or restoring them for riding and not for putting them into a lifeless, static collection. More so than any other motorcycle, many have remained in the hands of their original owners, and it is still possible today to find them in such a state.

BMW looked after these customers for longer than any other company, and made nearly every spare part for the 1960s models available from the factory for years after the end of production. Then, just when this service seemed no longer possible or required, the increasing demand from classic bike enthusiasts forced a change of plans in Munich. Rather than abandon a lucrative and enthusiastic following, the spare parts supply and remanufacturing was continued by a northern German specialist company which supplies the official BMW dealer network. More parts from the 1950s models are returning to the shelves and can be ordered through local dealers in Germany and vintage BMW suppliers in the United States and England.

At the same time there are many independent operations throughout Germany, the United States and England with their own spare parts programs and their own remanufacturing, as well as a sizeable quantity of used parts. But a word of warning here: there can be the same problems with BMW as with replacement parts everywhere.

Riding a 1960 R60/2

The Earles-fork BMW Boxers were classics even before the end of their fifteen-year-long production run. Sedate tourers and perfect sidecar haulers, they were held in high esteem everywhere in the world. Expensive outside of Germany, they remained a dream for a lot of motorcyclists. When author Stefan Knittel had the chance to lay his hands on a running but not complete example in the early 1970s a quick deal was struck and the necessary work completed in record time. What a step up from a 250 cc DKW two-stroke to the big Boxer!

The R60/2 seems to always start on the first kick, due in large part to the low compression ratio.

The shutter on the air filter housing can then be opened, and the engine runs more freely with plenty of fresh air flowing in. The inevitable "clonk" is usually heard before the first gear is engaged. Letting in the clutch causes another sensation. At the same time as power comes through the driveshaft, the rear end of the BMW lifts, only to come down again when rolling forward.

The ride is like being on a cloud, with soft springing at the front end, the rear and the middle. The single-spring rubber saddle, together with the swing-arm suspension, provided armchair comfort, which was alright on rough road surfaces, but gave an uncertain feel for the road as soon as speed was increased. It should be noted, however, that this was the way BMW intended it. Only a young aspiring sports rider did not want to know about it, and was not able to appreciate the soft ride on short hauls. It was the long-distance rider who really liked BMW's offerings.

The official performance figure of 30 PS seemed to be an understatement from the factory for the 594 cc engine feels much more powerful. Maybe it is the general character of the R60/2 that made it seem more powerful, but it nevertheless accelerated well despite the heavy gearchange action. More than 80 mph appears on the clock with no effort at all, even on a short straight. The accompanying exhaust note remains subdued as one would expect from such a gentleman's motorcycle.

Steering was a bit on the firm and heavy side with the Earles-type swing-arm front end, but it shows a large advantage under heavy braking with no front-end at all. The only thing that moves up and down is the rear end when you open or close the throttle. One has to get used to that as well as to the riding position, which is a bit too far forward. Gone is the sitting-in-the-bike feel of the earlier models; you sit high up on the mount. The standard handlebars are too narrow to allow easy and at the same time quick and positive handling in comparison to sports models with less weight. Though this does not imply that there were any faults with the general roadholding abilities of the R60/2, it is just different, but nevertheless surefooted in the long run.

Not all police bikes were Harleys, at least not in North Miami Beach in the late 1960s. These BMWs were available with a 12 volt electrical system and lights of your choice. The one on the left is fitted with twin blue-lens Hella spotlamp mirrors, which today would sell for a small fortune at a flea market. *Vintage BMW Bulletin, Richard Kahn*

Beauty attracts beauty, they say. In this case it is our very own Miss BMW of 1968 at the Daytona races on an R60/2. *Daytona International Speedway*

There are inferior-quality parts among the increasing number of parts becoming available, especially when the country of origin is no longer Germany.

As for finding complete machines, recently the German market seems to be flooded with R50 models, for which there is a simple explanation. The French police and armed forces are retiring more and more of their twenty-five- to thirty-year-old BMWs—and there are still a lot of them to come, as there are a surprisingly large number still on duty. They can be had in varying condition, but few have seen an easy life of limited mileage. They can either be bought as restoration projects or ready for the road after a basic overhaul through some specialist garages in Germany. The 26 PS workhorse can be a

good buy as it is not expensive compared to other 500s from the period; it is also easy to restore an R50 to factory-fresh condition as there are spare parts readily available. But as might be expected, the factory spares are not cheap and even reproduction parts are becoming very expensive.

Ratings

The most coveted collectors model undoubtedly is the R68, of which there were only 1,452 built between 1952 and 1954. Its performance should not be tried to the limit under today's traffic conditions, but it is a five-star motorcycle even when standing still.

Not quite so highly rated are the other sports models, with the R69 and the R50S having the bonus of being very rare. Still, their practical qualities as useable classics for the road put them into the same league as all the other BMW models of that period. The extra performance of the R69S alone does not warrant a higher rating as enough of the

By 1968 prices had crept up a bit, but the basic 500 cc twin cost only $108 more than it had sold for in 1951—eighteen years earlier! *Vintage BMW Bulletin, Richard Kahn*

more than 11,000 machines produced over a period of nine years are still available.

The high-performance R50S should be approached with caution. Although a mere 1,634 were built, there had to be a reason why such a high-revving 500 should have a short production life. With the benefit of hindsight, the culprit seems to be the over-stressed crankshaft. Rare indeed is the R50S which has managed to avoid a major rebuild. All the more reason to be wary, unless it can be proven that the machine has either just undergone such a repair, or that it has led a sheltered, low-mileage life in the hands of a conservative owner who never ran the bike

at its limit. To be sure, a low production figure adds somewhat to its inherent value, but all that is of little worth if the machine cannot be ridden because of a recent, or impending, engine failure.

Nevertheless, the sports models are considerably more expensive than the touring models, although in the United States most prices seem to have remained equal and relatively stable for the last ten years. Still, the 1950s and 1960s Boxers all rate in the four-star bracket. Interesting factory-fitted extras, or even well-known aftermarket accessories, of which there have been quite a few in Germany as well as in the United States, can add to the value, as they have always

Last of the line, this 600 cc R60US still has the basic 1955 frame, tank and engine design, but sports the new US telescopic forks, which found little favor at the time of introduction among the diehard Earles-fork devotees. Today, a US fork twin such as this usually commands a lesser price than its Earles-fork sibling, possibly purely for aesthetic reasons. *Vintage BMW Bulletin, Guy de la Rupelle*

been in high regard by BMW buyers. However, beware; they have to be the genuine period articles.

This applies also to sidecars. The factory-offered Steib TR500 combinations are preferred to other outfits, even though the S series bullet-shaped Steib bodies do fit the style of an R67/2 or R51/3. Modern plastic sidecars are to be avoided, as they are not in character with the period.

As a result of the recent developments in demand, the division into two distinctive groups can be made. The plunger-frame R51/2, R51/3, R67 and R68 are mainly bought by collectors, whereas the Earles-fork range still appeals to the rider as well, with a wide range of prices making a first buy easy.

Chapter 4

Singles
1925–1966

Model	Years	Type	Rating
R39	1925–1927	250 cc ohv	★★★★★
R2	1931–1936	200 cc ohv	★★★
R4	1932–1937	400 cc ohv	★★★
R3	1936	300 cc ohv	★★★
R35	1937–1940	350 cc ohv	★★★
R20	1937–1938	200 cc ohv	★★
R23	1938–1940	250 cc ohv	★★
R24	1948–1950	250 cc ohv	★★
R25	1950–1951	250 cc ohv	★★★
R25/2	1951–1954	250 cc ohv	★★★
R25/3	1953–1956	250 cc ohv	★★★
R26	1956–1960	250 cc ohv	★★★
R27	1960–1966	250 cc ohv	★★★

The first BMW motorcycle, the R32, available from 1923 on, was one of the most expensive models on the market, so consequently production goals were never too optimistic. On the other hand, the company's management was not interested in small-scale motorcycle production as their only business. The motorcycle side was intended to earn the money to help establish

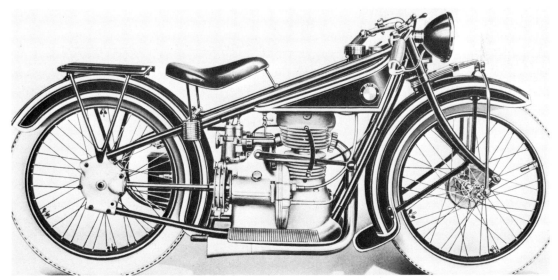

The first single-cylinder BMW was the R39 of 1925, a 250 cc ohv sports model, which had already been upgraded with a rear driveshaft brake, a benefit the flat-twin R32 still lacked.

Very few R39s survive today. Finding one will most likely get you a call or letter from the BMW Museum in Munich!

A success from the start, the 200 cc R2 was introduced in 1931. It is shown in the Series I version with exposed valve gear and an ugly humpbacked gas tank. Early examples of the R2 are quite scarce today.

new projects in the aircraft engine field, and possibly aid in the development of a BMW automobile. It was therefore inevitable that BMW had to increase motorcycle sales by expanding the range of models. Together with the sports mount R37, a new single-cylinder design was aimed toward the less wealthy customer, at a lower price than being asked for the flat twins.

Prewar singles

The 250 cc ohv single-cylinder R39 was first shown at the Berlin Motor Show in December 1924, a mere eight months after development work had begun. It took, however, another nine months to reach the market as there were still quite a few problems to be overcome. Upon closer inspection it was easy to see that this was not going to be a low-price volume-production model to compete with other ride-to-work motorcycles. The engine was again mounted longitudinally in the frame, which also was of a twin-tube design. The three-speed gearbox was bolted directly to the crankcase and driven through a single-plate dry clutch mounted to the flywheel. The rear-wheel drive was by shaft as on the Boxers. The upper half of the crankcase incorporated a

cylinder barrel within the same casting, bearing larger fins than the Boxer barrels. A cast-iron liner was shrunk into the alloy band. The alloy cylinder head with its one-piece valve cover came from the R37 sports Boxer, for the cylinder dimensions were unchanged at 68x68 mm for bore and stroke.

Year and model	1925–1927 R39
Engine	Overhead-valve single cylinder
Bore and stroke	68x68 mm
Displacement	247 cc
Horsepower	6.5 PS at 4000 rpm
Carburetion	Single BMW two-lever type, 20 mm
Ignition	Bosch magneto
Lubrication	Wet sump
Gearbox	Three-speed, hand actuated
Clutch	Single disc, dry
Frame	Twin tube
Suspension	Leading-link leaf-sprung front forks; rigid rear
Brakes	Drum brake at the front wheel; contracting band on driveshaft drum
Wheels and tires	20 in. wheels; 27x3.5 in. beaded-edge tires
Wheelbase	48.5 in.
Weight	242.5 lb. dry
Seat height	28.3 in.
Top speed	60 mph

The engine output was remarkably good for the time. The official 6.5 PS at 4000 rpm was regarded as rather conservative as the 250 ran up to 60 mph with no special tuning required. Thus it was not a big surprise for the development engineers at the BMW factory when Sepp Stelzer won the 1925 German road racing championship in the 250 cc class on an R39. Meanwhile, most teething troubles seemed to have been solved, and the model went on sale from September on, albeit at a much higher price than first expected. Complete with the Bosch magneto-generator lighting set and speedometer, it cost 2,150 German Marks, which was only 50 Marks less than the basic side-valve flat-twin R32.

Sales were good during the first few months but soon dwindled in 1926, and in addition the factory now heard from their dealers about some serious technical shortcomings. Rapid wear in the cylinder bore led to unacceptable oil consumption, which could only be stopped by furnishing new specially hardened liners. Then a problem with a slackening fit within the alloy barrel-cum-crankcase could not be solved with total success. Production of the first single-cylinder BMW came to a halt by the end of 1926 after only 855 units, with the remaining stock not sold off until well into 1927.

When BMW tried their hands at a single-cylinder setup for the second time, they had learned their lesson. The German laws concerning vehicle taxes and driver's licences had been changed after April 1, 1928, and all vehicles up to 200 cc could be used without having to pay a tax or procure a driver's licence. The machines only had to be properly registered and third-party insurance was compulsory. This opened up the German market for mass-produced inexpensive motorcycles with DKW, the two-stroke specialists from Zschopau, claiming the lion's share. BMW was not interested at first, concentrating on their large-capacity flat twins, but with the worsening of the economic climate after the Wall Street Crash, the Munich directors had to revise their thinking, as more and more people found it impossible to buy an expensive motorcycle. A 200 cc BMW would have a tough time competing with the basic two-stroke models from the other manufacturers; it also could not be more expensive than the four-stroke competition. It was no easy task for the BMW designers to find a compromise between the traditional high BMW standards and a price that could attract buyers even when money was tight.

Again, there had to be a shaft-drive layout for the new R2 model, so the single-cylinder engine was mounted longitudinally into the frame with a three-speed gearbox bolted to the rear of the engine. The power unit consisted of a one-piece barrel-shaped crankcase, onto which a cast-iron cylinder was now bolted. The cylinder head was cast in light alloy with deep vertical fins but the overhead valves were not enclosed as had been previous practice. Only the rocker arms on the pushrod side worked in a separate housing, with the pushrods running inside chrome-plated tubes. Lubrication was by oil mist from the crankcase which flowed up these tubes; there was a third tube in between the others where excess oil dribbled back down. The built-up crankshaft ran in a ball bearing at the rear and a shell bearing at the front end, which had to be pressure-lubricated directly from the oil pump. The timing chain which drove the camshaft and the generator was kept in tension by turning the generator in its fitting clip on the left-hand side of the engine. The contact breaker for the coil ignition system was located under a separate housing outside of the timing cover on the front. With a compression ratio of 6.7:1 and a 19 mm Sum needle-jet carburetor, 6 PS at 3500 rpm was reached for the 198 cc engine, which had a bore and stroke of 63x64 mm.

Frame and forks on the R2 were quite similar in design to that of the R11 and R16 Boxer models, being made out of channel-section pressed steel; the main differences were the dimensions and the wall thickness of the material. The same sort of pinstriping was applied to the frame but the gas tank gained a distinctive blue top panel over the otherwise black paint job. The engine was offset to the right in the frame to provide a direct driveline in top gear from the crankshaft to the rear-wheel pinion. To counterbalance this, the electric horn, large battery

The valve gear of the R2 gained a cover in 1932, and this 1934 Series III already has an enclosed generator and Amal carburetor. Tools are still in a separate tin box behind the engine. That massive low front fender brace is actually a front prop stand, useful when changing a tire.

Pressed-steel frame cousins: two 1936 BMWs at the US Vintage Club's Massachusetts meet in 1983. In the foreground, a 200 cc R2 single from New York, flanked by a 750 cc ohv, 80 mph R16, flown up by a true enthusiast in his private plane from Virginia. *Vintage BMW Bulletin, Marie Lacko*

and large toolbox were situated on the left. Light alloy footboards were used again. The gear lever was of a distinctive pattern; as on a car, it was a long rod protruding from the gearbox top towards the right-hand side of the gas tank. It did not work in an external gate but on a ball mechanism on the selector. The BMW R2 was numbered in a logical manner for the first time based on engine capacity. The bike was no lightweight at 242 lb. dry, but the performance did not really suffer and the top speed was in the 55 mph bracket.

When it became available from spring 1931 on, it sold well from the start, even better than BMW had expected. The price was three times that of the cheapest DKW but also less than half of the 750 ohv BMW R16, which made it exactly right as a beginner's BMW. There were no technical problems reported, and customers received the expected well-designed, reliable mount for their money.

After 4,260 units had been built, the first large change led to the Series II R2 in mid 1932, with the cylinder head now topped by

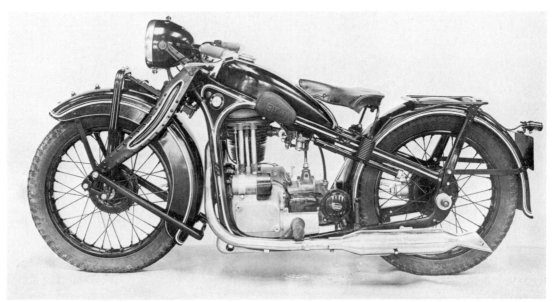

The trusty R4 in Series IV form with a redesigned crankcase incorporating the tool compartment, which was located in the gearbox case before. The battery now sat in a pocket in the gearbox casting, and the kickstarter has moved from the rear to the right side of the gearbox, where it was kicked rearward, like on all the "normal" motorcycles of the day.

the familiar one-piece cover. At the same time, a German-made Amal carburetor was introduced. In 1934 the valve openings were timed differently by a newly designed camshaft; this led to an increase in engine power to 8 PS at 4500 rpm. The generator on the left-hand side of the engine also gained a light-alloy cover.

The next improvement for the Series IV R2 of 1935 added a friction damper with scissors action to the leaf-spring front fork, a reshaped, longer gas tank, a new type of headlamp from Bosch and a rubber saddle instead of the old leatherette saddle.

The R2 was not the only single-cylinder BMW the Munich development engineers were working on at the beginning of the 1930s. The gap between the 200 cc single and the remaining 750 cc Boxers was to be filled by a new middleweight motorcycle. There, BMW opted for another single instead of a much more expensive new flat twin, and when the new 400 cc ohv R4 went on sale in early 1932 it looked similar to the R2. The rolling chassis remained virtually identical, as only a few strengthening flat

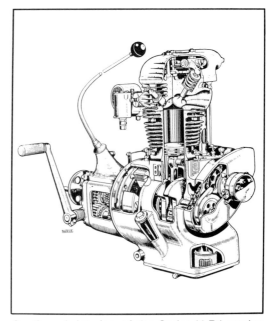

Sectioned drawing of the Series V R4 engine with the timing chain running parallel to the rubber V-belt that spun the generator. As with all BMWs, the oil filler plug incorporated a dipstick.

steel strips had been riveted into the main section of the forks. The front mudguard gained side valances and the tires were of a wider section. The engine was based on the R2 design but with an enlarged 78 mm cylinder bore and 84 mm stroke. The R4 engine also used the enclosed cylinder head from the start. A horizontal Sum three-jet carburetor was mounted and the power output for the 400 cc engine was rated at 12 PS at a mere 3500 rpm.

The BMW R4 was intended to cater to a new segment in the motorcycle market. It could not compete against the ohv 500s of its day, and was more in the league of the side-valve workhorses where it showed some advantages with a more modern engine and shaft drive. For the Series II R4 of 1933, the styling became even more attractive with a new four-speed gearbox and fashionable rubber-covered footrests instead of the light-alloy boards. The improved cylinder head brought a further 2 PS in 1934, the left-hand side of the engine was tidied up

with the generator now under a cover and the toolbox incorporated into the gearbox casting. This was changed again in 1935 when the toolbox was integrated into the crankcase, the generator resituated on top of that and now driven by a V-belt, and the battery set into a box of its own alongside the gearbox.

A rugged motorcycle, the R4 was still not that popular with younger buyers, although they gained good riding experience on it when being trained for military or police service, for the BMW R4 was used in large numbers by the army and other forces in Germany. In the hands of talented staff riders and the works team, the R4 was used extensively in German trials events. It was in fact at one time offered as an off-road sports model in the BMW catalog without any alterations from the standard model.

A short-lived model in the BMW singles range was the R3 of 1936, a small-bore (68 mm) 305 cc counterpart to the R4. It was intended for certain markets where 300s

Used as the standard training and dispatch rider model by military and police forces in Germany, the R4 was renowned for its reliability. The right-hand front fork leg now has a friction damper. Clearly seen here on this 1935 Series IV R4 is the rearward-swinging kickstarter and the steel crankcase "bash plate."

Year and model	1931–1936 R2
Engine	Overhead-valve single cylinder
Bore and stroke	63x64 mm
Displacement	198 cc
Horsepower	6 PS at 3500 rpm; 8 PS at 4500 rpm from 1934 on
Carburetion	Single Sum needle-jet type, 19 mm; Amal from 1933 on
Ignition	Coil
Lubrication	Wet sump
Gearbox	Three-speed, hand actuated
Clutch	Single disc, dry
Frame	Twin loop pressed-steel section
Suspension	Leading-link leaf-sprung front forks; rigid rear
Brakes	Drum brakes front and rear
Wheels and tires	19 in. wheels; 25x3 in. wire-type tires
Wheelbase	52 in.
Weight	242.5 lb. dry
Seat height	26.4 in.
Top speed	58 mph

were preferred to a 250 or a bigger model, but it wasn't a success for BMW and after a production run of only 740 units, it was dropped at the end of the same year.

The R4 itself was replaced in 1937 by an updated version called the R35, which had a smaller engine capacity. This time the cylinder bore was reduced to 72 mm to give a 342 cc capacity, but with a higher compression ratio the output remained at 14 PS. Together with the 350 cc version of the Series V R4 engine everything else other than the front forks was as before. The major innovation on the R35 was the telescopic front forks, although they were of a less-elaborate pattern than on the R5 Boxer because they had to make do without the hydraulic damper valves of the popular twin.

The BMW R35, like its predecessor, was bought in large numbers by the German military authorities and became the backbone of their motorcycle fleet for dispatch riding purposes, as well as for their thorough train-

Reducing the engine capacity from 398 to 342 cc and fitting undamped telescopic front forks with a redesigned front fender transformed the R4 into the new R35 in 1937. The model pictured here is the military version with leather pannier cases and a canvas-and-leather blackout cover over the headlamp.

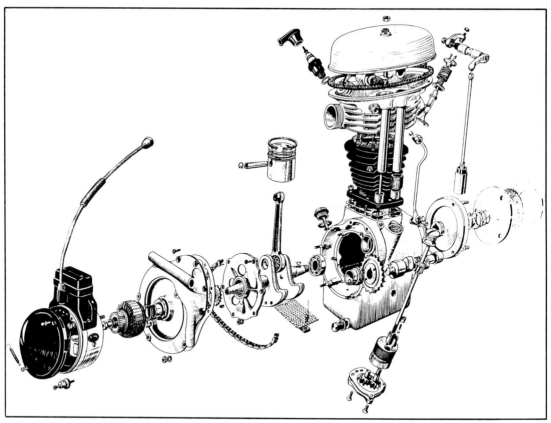

An exploded view of the redesigned 200 cc single-cylinder R20 of 1937–38.

ing courses. More than 15,000 units of the R4 were produced between 1932 and 1937, followed by the same number of the R35, built until 1940. There was even a small production run in 1947–48 behind the Iron Curtain when the Soviet supervisors in East Germany ordered the former BMW car plant at Eisenach to use up old stocks of parts, which was followed with a modified version of the R35 having plunger rear suspension and called the EMW (Eisenacher Motoren Werke), until production ceased in the early 1950s.

With the new generation of Boxers such as the R5 available from 1936 on, the old-fashioned singles were no longer in much demand by civilian buyers. There was no reason to change the dated R4 and R35, but the smaller R2 model was completely redesigned in due course. It appeared in early

1937 as the R20 with a modified 200 cc engine in a new tubular frame. The engine dimensions were changed to 60x68 mm bore and stroke, while the power output remained at 8 PS. From its side position, the generator was moved to the front of the timing cover where it was driven directly by the crankshaft. The gearbox also looked much more tidy, but it still had only three speeds, which were now engaged by a foot lever on the left side.

The frame of the R20 was a rather simple affair with butted-end tubes bolted in place. There was a single top tube under the new saddle gas tank with the toolbox on top, and twin downtubes that went around under the engine and back to the rear wheel. Two tubes also connected the top tube to the rear wheel mounting plates. The telescopic front forks were of the undamped type as on the

70

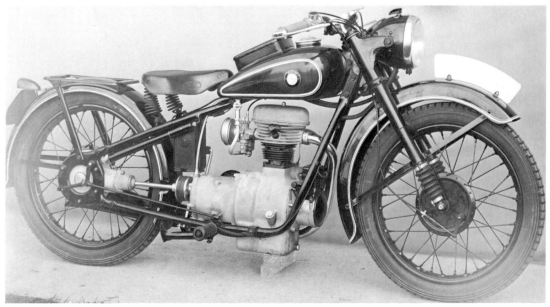

The 1937–38 R20 used a bolted-up tubular frame with simple undamped forks and a huge toolbox on top of the tiny gas tank. Along with an excellent set of tools, all BMWs came with a truly magnificent tire pump, one of the hardest items to find in its original form when restoring a prewar BMW today.

R35. The D-section fenders had no pinstriping on the production models; only the prototypes of the R20 used them in photographs. The new 200 looked to be lighter than the R2 but the official figure was 286 lb. This did not harm its performance, which was on par with the popular two-strokes of the same capacity from the other German manufacturers.

Year and model	1937–1940 R35
Engine	Overhead-valve single cylinder
Bore and stroke	72x84 mm
Displacement	342 cc
Horsepower	14 PS at 4500 rpm
Carburetion	Single Sum three-jet type, 22 mm
Ignition	Coil
Lubrication	Wet sump
Gearbox	Four-speed, hand actuated
Clutch	Single disc, dry
Frame	Twin loop pressed-steel section
Suspension	Telescopic front forks; rigid rear
Brakes	Drum brakes front and rear
Wheels and tires	3.50x19 in.
Wheelbase	51 in.
Weight	342 lb.
Seat height	28 in.
Top speed	60 mph

After a production run of 5,000 motorcycles, a change was forced upon BMW like every other company by the new traffic laws in Germany in effect after June 1938. No longer were the 200s excepted from the licence regulations, and a new restricted driver's license was introduced for all vehicles up to 250 cc. BMW responded by increasing the engine capacity to 247 cc with the introduction of a new cylinder barrel together with a 68 mm piston. The power thus went up to 10 PS and the new model was called the R23. The only difference between it and the R20 concerned the gas tank, where the toolbox was now sunk into the tank's top. With no less than 6,011 units produced in 1939 alone, the R23 set a new record for BMW, but the outbreak of World War II changed everything. The last 1,000 R23s from 1940 did not go into the hands of civilian buyers, ending up instead with the military.

Postwar singles

It was at the 1948 Geneva Motor Show that BMW announced its comeback into the field of motorcycle manufacturers after some

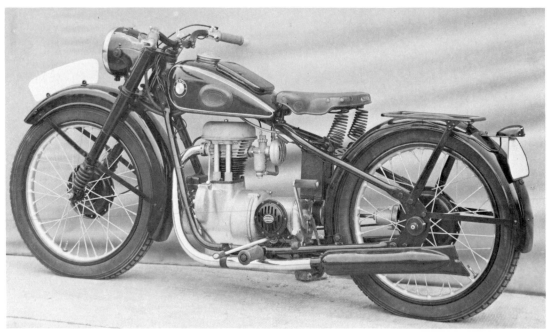

The built-in toolbox on the gas tank distin-
guishes the R23 from the R20, which is what
they called the 250 cc version available from
1938 to 1940.

The first postwar BMW was the R24, based on
the old R23 but with an updated engine design.
The R24 was built in the years 1948–50.

doubt about its future prospects in the immediate postwar years. The only new product BMW could present was the R24 with an updated 250 cc single-cylinder engine in the old R23 frame, of which the first were built nine months later, starting in December 1948. The engine design was influenced by the R75 in several details, with the rockers no longer working in cast-in bosses but on pillars, which were bolted on. The pushrods were led in through tunnels in the cylinder head and the valve covers were two separate pieces held down by a clamp with a single central bolt. A change in the valve angle and a higher compression of 6.75:1 together with a new 22 mm Bing carburetor increased the power output to 12 PS at 5600 rpm. Also new was a four-speed gearbox and the electrical equipment from the Noris company of Nuremberg. The finish was brightened by pinstriping on the fenders and a chromed fishtail muffler, but the wheels lost their silver-grey center band and spokes, and were now painted a solid black.

Sales were promising from the start, and 9,400 of the R24s left the Munich factory in 1949 alone. With the German motorcycle industry getting back in stride, quite a number of modern utility two-strokes appeared on the market. These two-strokes and some well-known models that were put back in production, such as the Zündapp 200 or the British-looking 250 four-stroke NSU, were all less expensive to buy than the BMW. But the R24 held a position of its own in the market, as it carried the famous blue-and-white BMW roundel on the tank. In the light of the latest racing success on the German scene, every BMW owner felt even more proud of his or her decision to pay more money for a much more prestigious motorcycle. From a much-improved corporate financial position, further technical developments could be envisaged for 1950 for the singles as well as the reborn flat-twin models.

Only minor modifications were felt necessary for the single-cylinder engine, such as a beefed-up crankshaft and an inlet valve enlarged by 2 mm, together with a greater inlet port and increased choke size for the

The first postwar BMW ad in an American magazine. The March 1949 issue of *The Motorcyclist* showed this R24 of 250 cc, a virtual copy of the prewar R23. In all likelihood, the R23 never had the opportunity to get to the United States prior to the outbreak of the war in 1939. *Vintage BMW Bulletin, Oscar Fricke*

carburetor. The latter measures, however, were maintained for one season only, before the previous sizes were reintroduced. Much more important was the new frame for the R25 that made its debut in September 1950 as the successor to the R24. The most significant innovation concerned the long-awaited plunger rear suspension, and the frame tubes, which were now welded together to provide a stronger chassis more suitable for attaching a sidecar. A valanced front fender with an elegant sweeping tail added to the modern appearance.

The R25/2 replaced the R25 during 1951 with the engine modifications, although the rest of the model changed in only a few

On the 1948 R24 a new cylinder head with split valve covers was used, which were continued up through the R27 of 1966.

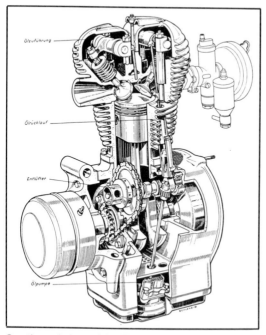

Sectioned view of the R24 engine, of which only small details were to be changed over the next 18 years. The R24 produced 12 PS, but with increases in compression ratio, the R27 of 1966 reached 18 PS.

respects. The front fender stay now went over the top on the outside and the pinstripe pattern no longer followed around the edge but followed the contour of a narrower sports fender. Again, a new type of saddle was used, the simple old rubber seat was replaced by a new single-spring swinging seat, which was now of a more elaborate construction with a horizontal coil spring activated by a lever arm that was all built into the new seat frame.

Success for the 250 BMW was assured, even against many new competitors, such as the many equally powerful and refined two-strokes, or the 18 PS NSU Max with its overhead-camshaft engine and a swing-arm rear suspension. The reliability and the quality of a motorcycle from the Munich factory was still regarded as superior.

BMW did not disappoint its followers when yet another update of the R25 theme was made ready for the Frankfurt Motorcycle Show in October 1953. A new shape for the gas tank, new telescopic forks at the front, full-width hubs and alloy wheel rims distinguished the new R25/3 from the R25/2. But as could be expected, there had been a

The R24, when treated to a new chassis of welded-steel tubing and plunger rear suspension, as well as a redesigned seat, became the R25 of 1950.

In the 1950s, the 250 cc BMW was a popular sidecar machine. Here an R25 is mated to a lightweight Steib LS200.

great deal of detail work put into the new model—more than first met the eye. Starting with the rolling chassis, the new 18 in. wheels that replaced the older 19 in. wheels were intended to give a more comfortable ride, and the redesigned front forks now incorporated hydraulic-damping action as on the Boxer models.

The new gas tank had become flatter and longer to accommodate the front mount of the seat and close up the ugly gap found there. The toolbox lid went from the top to the left-hand side of the gas tank where it was covered by the rubber knee grip. The main reason for changing the gas tank was based on a more important technical innovation. A long, curved induction pipe was built into the right half of the tank leading to the air filter at the front of it and connected to the carburetor at the other end by a rubber hose. With this system, it is easy to see why this larger gas tank still held only 12 liters or 3 gallons of fuel.

The induction system was part of a fine-tuning program designed to provide a simultaneous increase in engine power and reliability. This was achieved by various means,

BMW cheesecake, complete with 1951 R25 single. The two-color rim paint, black generator cover and an overall lack of unnecessary chrome are details often overlooked by well-meaning but overzealous restorers. *Vintage BMW Bulletin, Richard Kahn*

Detail improvements made the R25 into the R25/2 during 1951. The new model could be recognized by the different pinstriping scheme and a bolt-on versus riveted front fender stay. A redesigned seat spring, similar to the R51 and R67 twins, was also used.

Riding a 1950 R25

The 250 cc BMW was the Volkswagen Beetle of the two-wheeled world. A common sight on German roads until the early 1970s, the BMW single was the motorcycle nearly every rider had learned on. When they were no longer wanted one could get them at a low price or even free, like the way my brother acquired his 1950 model. His had a red frame with the fenders and gas tank painted white, but all parts were still the original ones and the mechanical condition was quite good.

Provided the battery is in good condition, the R25 is a good starter and one or two hefty swings on the kickstart are enough to bring the single-cylinder engine to life. It doesn't start with a roar, but with a gentle plonking noise instead, and like every BMW with longitudinal crankshaft the sideways rotation can be felt as the whole motorcycle tries to incline itself to the right. The gearchange is as on the twins—heavy and loud. As more revs are needed for any sort of reasonable acceleration from standstill, an immediate surprise is the building up of a lot of vibration—something one is not used to in a BMW, until one has tried a single-cylinder model, that is.

The ratios of the first three gears seem to be rather high and give an impression of a hard-pressed engine. This changes, however, in top gear where the R25 could run all day long with the typical low single-cylinder beat. Trying to gather more speed reveals the small-capacity engine that sounds like a 500 but remains a 250 with only 12 hard-working horsepower on tap. As soon as more than 40 mph are reached, the exhaust noise, together with a good deal more vibration, makes the ride less pleasant. Still, nearly 60 mph can be attained under most conditions.

Considering its role as a ride-to-work mount in the less dense traffic of past decades, the R25 must be rated as a much more desirable motorcycle than the much cheaper two-strokes often built out of commonly available components by other manufacturers. Today it has to be taken into account that this is a different BMW from the famous flat-twin models—and not only because of the engine. The undamped telescopic front forks can cope with a smooth road surface, but tend to bounce up and down on anything else, and they all wear out rather quickly. The same could be said about the plunger rear suspension. As there is not a great deal of wheel travel on both ends the handling is not appreciably affected.

The riding position is quite good with the small tank comfortably nestled between the legs, but a worn out front mount of the saddle can be annoying as there is only one vertical compression spring, not the clever horizontal lever setup as on the Boxer models. Whenever the handling seems to be affected the problem can be put down to the seat mount in most cases. The 160 mm drum brakes do work surprisingly well compared to other motorcycles from the same period, with strong alloy back plates not allowing for any distortion.

A troublefree motorcycle that needed much less service work than most other models, the BMW single always held a special position on the motorcycle market and it is attractive today as an affordable classic that can still be used without great limitations.

---

such as the controlled flow of intake air, together with a better muffler for the exhaust system, a higher compression ratio of 7.0:1 and the larger 24 mm carburetor, made either by Bing or Sawe. Tests with a special black paint on the cylinder head afforded much better heat dissipation and it was applied to the production models from then on. The new official horsepower figure was a conservative 13 PS at 5800 rpm; later tests revealed it was more like 14 PS at 6500 rpm, which explained the top speed of more than 70 mph.

Over the winter the old R25/2 was still available from stock alongside the new R25/3 but during 1954 the new model took over completely with no less than 25,355 units produced in that year alone. But now, the peak had been reached for the German motorcycle market, and as a ride-to-work vehicle a small car or a 50 cc moped came to be preferred. Sales dwindled rapidly and soon one motorcycle manufacturer after the other was forced to close its doors. BMW was caught in the middle of the modernization of their models with the Earles-type

Year and model	1953–1956 R25/3
Engine	Overhead-valve single cylinder
Bore and stroke	68x68 mm
Displacement	247 cc
Horsepower	13 PS at 5800 rpm
Carburetion	Single Bing, 24 mm
Ignition	Coil
Lubrication	Wet sump
Gearbox	Four-speed, foot actuated
Clutch	Single disc, dry
Frame	Twin tube
Suspension	Telescopic front forks; plunger rear
Brakes	Drum brakes front and rear
Wheels and tires	3.25x18 in.
Wheelbase	53.7 in.
Weight	330 lb.
Seat height	29 in.
Top speed	74 mph

front forks and a swing-arm rear suspension introduced for the flat twins at the beginning of 1955. A similar concept was prepared for the 250 as well as further modifications to the engine.

Available from early 1956 on, the R26 had already been produced in sufficient numbers in the autumn of the previous year. There were large stocks of the plunger-framed R25/3 to be cleared and as the old model was cheaper than its R26 successor, it still sold well enough to require a further batch of nearly 500 units to be added during the year. The R26 without doubt was worth the difference in price if only for the superior handling and comfort of the new suspension that was matched by the increased engine output. Larger cooling fins on the cylinder head made the black paint redundant and provided enough heat dissipation at an even higher compression ratio. Together with a 26 mm carburetor and a more efficient paper-element air filter in the box under the saddle where the battery was stored, an output of 15 PS at 6400 rpm was announced for the 250 cc engine. The gas tank once again had the toolbox lid on the top, and held 15

This diminutive 250 cc 1953 R25/2 was ridden 180 miles to one of the Ohio meets in 1983 by proud owner Terry Baxter, who had restored it in less than a year's time from a pile of neglected bits. *Vintage BMW Bulletin, Rich Scheckler*

liters or 4 gallons of fuel. With its dry weight of just under 350 lb., the R26 could reach 80 mph.

During 1956 the R26 sold comparatively well with quite a lot of the production going abroad, in particular to Third-World countries. The 250 cc BMW was the only German motorcycle that left the factory in numbers between 4,000 and 5,000 in these lean years towards the end of the 1950s, but even this constant production run was a drastic drop from previous successful levels. But, thanks to the increasing percentage of export sales, further development efforts were still affordable alongside the growing automotive commitments of the company. Lacking the funds for new designs, methodical refinements and a search for a slightly higher power output became the order of the day.

Against these limitations BMW came up with quite an interesting concept for its single-cylinder model. The engine power had reached 18 PS at a high 7400 rpm by means of a higher compression ratio and new valve opening times through a new camshaft, the contact breaker set had been repositioned onto the front end of the camshaft and the timing chain gained a spring-

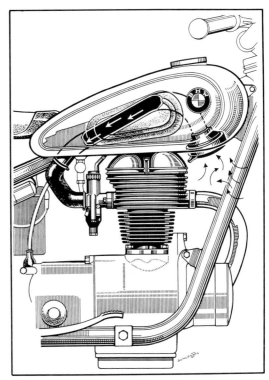

Cold air was drawn into the carburetor through a long tube that ran under the gas tank on the R25/3, all part of the new engine tuning scheme.

A major updating brought the R25/3 in 1953. New front forks and full-width hubs, alloy rims, larger gas tank and improved carburetion were all featured.

The Steib sidecar could be ordered through BMW together with the R25/3 as a complete outfit and was listed in the catalogs as the BMW Standard sidecar, which had only minor differences in trim, lighting and insignia from its Steib LS200 counterpart.

A comfortable chassis with swing-arm suspension for both front and rear wheels and a higher engine output were the features of the R26. Note that at last the stubby hand-shift neutral finder has been eliminated, but that the cast boss where it used to be attached still remained.

loaded slipper tensioner. Unfortunately, increased vibration and a rougher power delivery would have put the engine in conflict with the soft-sprung, comfortable chassis; the only answer therefore was to introduce rubber insulation between frame and engine. This had been tried on a number of motorcycles before but without much success. Simply mounting the engine and gearbox unit on four rubber buffers bolted to the frame was found not to be enough, so an additional cylinder head bracket with harder rubber to limit its movement, and two fore-and-aft buffers on the front and at the rear of the block to keep the longitudinal travel under control, had to be added to the setup.

The debut of the new R27 was overshadowed by the new sporting R50S and R69S Boxers, which appeared at the same time in autumn 1960, but in terms of projected production figures the 250 cc single was considered the most important model. This planning, however, proved to be wrong as early as 1961 when the new Boxers began to sell increasingly well, especially in the United States. In this lucrative export market big powerful motorcycles were in demand, as well as cheap, small-sized runabouts. The R27 was too expensive for what it was, though, with the Japanese and Italian factories flooding the US market with models up to 250 cc that had real sporting pedigrees and could deliver a performance to match at competitive prices.

The days were over for a sedate and unpretentious motorcycle that was built to last, and which was noted for its comfortable ride instead of its sporting looks. In 1966 BMW built a last run of 2,400 R27, many of which were still unsold toward the end of the following year. The history of the single-cylinder BMW models thus came to an end, and the prototype R28 project was halted soon thereafter when the German army, a prospective customer, decided not to adopt it, preferring the 125 cc Hercules two-stroke, which would replace their 10,000 Maico 250s then in use.

The new cylinder head with the increased fin area of the 15 PS 250 cc engine makes it easy to recognize this engine as belonging to the R26 of 1955–60.

More BMW cheesecake, complete with a 1955–60 R26, showing off—among other things—the side-swing kickstart. *Vintage BMW Bulletin, Richard Kahn*

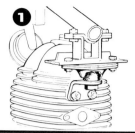

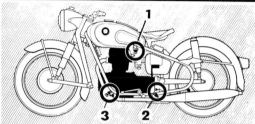

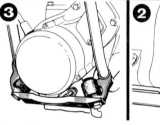

An elaborate system of rubber mounts between engine and frame was used only on the R27, which marked the final development of the BMW 250 cc ohv single-cylinder motorcycle.

Prospects

Not many of the prewar single-cylinder BMW models were sold outside Germany, especially as there were no special licensing or tax regulations for the 200 cc limit. But even today the R2 is not all that common in Germany. Of the 15,207 units that were produced between 1931 and 1936, most fell victim to neglect and the scrap drives of World War II. The same applies to the R20 and R23, which seem to be still rarer. The parts situation for these singles is therefore very limited.

The R4 and R35 models present a different story, however. About 15,000 of each left the Munich factory. Used in military service, they ended up on all fronts during World War II. Quite frequently they turn up today in places like Poland, where they have been in use for a long time since the war.

Year and model	1960–66 R27
Engine	Overhead-valve single cylinder
Bore and stroke	68x68 mm
Displacement	247 cc
Horsepower	18 PS at 7400 rpm
Carburetion	Single Bing, 26 mm
Ignition	Coil
Lubrication	Wet sump
Gearbox	Four-speed
Clutch	Single disc, dry
Frame	Twin tube
Suspension	Swing arm front and rear
Brakes	Drum brakes front and rear
Wheels and tires	3.25x18 in.
Wheelbase	54.3 in.
Weight	357 lb.
Seat height	30.3 in.
Top speed	81 mph

Surprisingly they still look original in most respects, even after being used for decades, but they are usually quite worn out mechanically. This is where the problems begin, because there are almost no new parts available, as a remanufacturing of replacement parts has not yet been undertaken. Used parts can be found, but in varying condition and more often than not too worn out to be useful. The situation might change in the future as the prewar singles are becoming increasingly popular, especially since they can still be bought for much less money than the flat twins, and consequently more of them are going to be restored than was previously thought possible.

The postwar range has always been popular, with good examples of R25/3, R26 or R27 models always in demand by various types of enthusiasts. Their legendary long-lasting qualities saw them in every day use in Germany sometimes well into the 1970s, when many young motorcycle enthusiasts with not much money began their hobby with the first rebuild of a 250 cc BMW. At one time the singles seemed to be the most popular beginners machines some twenty years after most of them had left the factory. Unfortunately, the easy availability and low cost of such machines, especially in Germany, made it easy for many an uncaring young owner to radically modify them, turning them into all sorts of abominations, from dirt bike to chopper. Consequently, most of the original parts were altered or discarded, making the restoration of many now an expensive proposition. Happily, interests have now changed, and those who still insist on improving their motorcycle with hacksaw and spray can generally choose a lesser machine, usually one with Oriental origins.

Outside Germany the 250s sold well in countries like Austria, Switzerland and the Netherlands, but everywhere else they were less popular than the Boxers and therefore today are harder to find, especially in the United States. As with all the BMW models there is always a good selection available in Germany, be it at swap meets or through the classifieds in the motorcycle magazines.

Those BMWs that remain to be resurrected by a new generation of enthusiasts have accounted for an increased demand for original and quality reproduction parts. As

It is not easy to tell this R27 from its predecessor, the R26, except for the obvious clue of not having a front top bolt mount on the engine block nor any attaching bosses welded to the frame on either side of the generator cover.

with the Boxers of the same period, quite a range of parts is now available through the official dealer network in Germany, or through various private suppliers in the United States.

Ratings

There is only one real five-star model among the single-cylinder motorcycles from BMW. The R39 from the 1920s is one of the rarest German motorcycles, in the same league as the R37 or an original racing BMW. It is nearly unobtainable as there are only a handful of them in the hands of members of the German BMW Veteranen Club who have little intention of selling them.

The next model is the R2 both in historical sequence and in the ratings, but not quite yet a four-star. It is, however, becoming increasingly popular among BMW enthusiasts.

Newcomers tend to prefer the larger-capacity R4, which is a good three-star motorcycle, with one in civilian finish preferred over a green- or tan-painted ex-Wehrmacht mount. The same applies more or less to the R35, but the curious pressed-steel leaf-spring front forks seem to prove more popular on the R4, than do the skinny telescopics of the R35.

Not much can be said about the R20 and R23, as they seem to appeal only to collectors who want to complete their range. Their significance on the market only warrants two stars at the moment. The same can be said about their postwar counterpart, the R24, the only difference being that the R24 can be found more easily, at least in Germany.

In the R25 series the main difference lies in the more practical aspects of the later models with their superior chassis and their higher popularity since the 1950s. The later R25/3 is the most desirable, even though the R25 and the R25/2 are the rarer ones. Three stars is the common rating for all of the R25 series, as well as for the Earles-fork R26 and R27.

From a practical standpoint regardless of purchase price, the R27 will probably become the mount of choice, since its rubber-mounted engine cancelled out most of the annoying vibration of the R26. It's also more practical as an everyday highway machine, again because of the smoother ride and better response of the accelerator-pump Bing carburetor, used near the end of the production run. The R27 tends to be more expensive as well, since only half as many were built compared to the R26.

A properly restored Bavarian Cream 1964 250 cc R27, last of the BMW singles. Generally, white BMWs—whether singles or flat twins—were delivered in Germany to highway patrol units or the fire departments, while dark green went to the local Polizei. Although there is no factory documentation stating that other colors were available to civilian customers, pre-1972 BMW motorcycles in colors other than black and Bavarian Cream do turn up throughout the world. In fact, the US importers, Butler & Smith, listed gas tanks or complete motorcycles in special colors as available in 1968, including two shades of white, one of red and even a dark blue or grey. Butler & Smith also imported cans of factory touch-up spray paint in the special colors, supporting the belief that other colors were available from BMW.

Chapter 5

Flat Twins 1969-On

Model	Years	Type	Rating
R50/5	1969–1973	500 cc ohv	★★★★
R60/5	1969–1973	600 cc ohv	★★★★
R75/5	1969–1973	750 cc ohv	★★★★
R60/6	1973–1976	600 cc ohv	★★★
R75/6	1973–1976	750 cc ohv	★★★
R90/6	1973–1976	900 cc ohv	★★★
R90S	1973–1976	900 cc ohv	★★★★
R60/7	1976–1980	600 cc ohv	★★★
R75/7	1976–1977	750 cc ohv	★★★
R80/7	1977–1986	800 cc ohv	★★★
R100/7	1976–1978	1000 cc ohv	★★★
R100S	1976–1978	1000 cc ohv	★★★
R100RS	1976–1984	1000cc ohv	★★★
R100RT	1978–1984	1000 cc ohv	★★★

After a long production run of fifteen years the last Earles-fork BMW models were built in the summer of 1969 and they were the last motorcycles to leave the Munich factory. The development of a new range of motorcycles had been concluded at the same time, but for these a completely new production line was installed in Berlin, where a former aircraft engine factory, that had been part of BMW's wartime operations and up until now produced an increasing number of car and motorcycle components, was enlarged and modernized. Back in Munich the rapidly expanding car production took up every square foot of the already crammed factory grounds, and moving the motorcycle plant away from Munich thus became inevitable. The administration and development offices remained situated in Munich, but complete production including foundry, frame building, machining, paint shop and assembly lines was concentrated at the Berlin Spandau plant from September 1969 on.

The new chassis had been seen before with the works International Six Days Trials team as early as 1963–64. The chassis featured the long-travel telescopic front forks that had become available on the R50US, R60US and R69US for the US market from 1967 to 1969. The frame again had a single large-diameter top tube and twin down-

A 750 cc Boxer BMW new in every detail made its debut in 1969 as the R75/5. Shown here is one from the first year, with low European bars and no side reflectors on the turn signal housings.

Model	Years	Type	Rating
R100CS	1980–1984	1000 cc ohv	★★★
R45	1978–1985	480 cc ohv	★★
R65	1978–1985	650 cc ohv	★★
R65LS	1981–1985	650 cc ohv	★★
R80G/S	1980–1987	800 cc ohv	★★★
R80RT	1982–1984	800 cc ohv	★★★
R80ST	1982 1984	800 cc ohv	★★★
R65	1985–on	650 cc ohv	★★★
R80	1984–on	800 cc ohv	★★★
R80RT	1984–on	800 cc ohv	★★★
R100RS	1986–on	1000 cc ohv	★★★
R100RT	1987–on	1000 cc ohv	★★★
R65GS	1988–on	650 cc ohv	★★★
R80GS	1987–on	800 cc ohv	★★★
R100GS	1988–on	1000 cc ohv	★★★

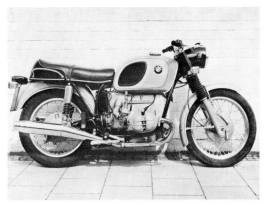

The big 24 liter or 6¼ gallon, gas tank and the kickup in the mufflers were typical features on the first /5 models, shown here on a 1969 R75/5.

bolted onto the main frame. The top brackets for the rear suspension units were welded to the rear loop. Wheel sizes were a larger 19 in. at the front but the usual 18 in. at the rear. The drum brakes, with the twin-leading-shoe at the front, remained unaltered as well.

The instrument cluster built in the /5 headlamp consisted of a speedometer, tachometer and indicator lights. Narrow handlebars were preferred by European buyers, while Americans got the higher ones. Still familiar to all owners of earlier models is the chrome and plastic key slide and cover, first introduced in 1953. The simple spike ignition key went back even farther, all the way to 1935, and could start any BMW.

tubes, with the latter no longer extended to the rear wheel but curved up to the top tube just behind the engine. With the gas tank hiding the single top tube, the design of the frame looked similar to the famous Norton Featherbed frame. The downtubes also crossed over the top tube on their way up to support the headstock on the top end, whereas the top tube was welded on at the bottom. Gusset plates were added to strengthen the steering head. The rear swing arm was mounted via the usual taper roller bearings into the lugs in the frame tubes and a pressed-steel bracket was welded on at each side to hold the mufflers and the passenger footrests. The rear part of the frame with the loop to support the seat and the struts running down to the muffler brackets was

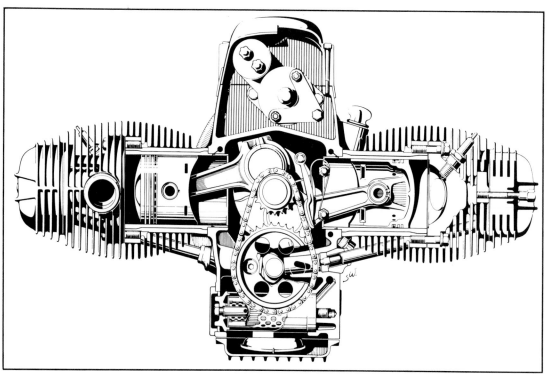

The repositioned camshaft below the crankshaft is clearly visible in this R75/5 engineering drawing. Plain bearing big ends were also new.

What nobody had seen before was the new engine with virtually everything new beyond the basic layout; the /5 engine was still a flat twin with overhead valves opened by pushrods. A single-disc dry clutch mounted into the car-type flywheel turned the bolted-on four-speed gearbox, and from there an enclosed shaft drive went to the bevel box of the rear-wheel drive. The engine and gearbox unit was much bigger than before with the slab-sided castings incorporating an electric starter motor on top of the crankcase and a built-in air filter case on top of the gearbox, the height of which filled the gap under the gas tank. The light-alloy crankcase was again of the one-piece-barrel type with the crankshaft inserted from the front. The new crankshaft was a one-piece forging with bolted-on counterweights instead of the earlier pressed-up assembly, and no longer ran in roller bearings. Shell bearings were now used fore and aft as well as on the crankshaft pins making split big ends necessary on the connecting rods. A high-pressure Eaton oil pump supplied the bearing surfaces, driven from the front end of the camshaft, which now ran below the crankshaft and was connected to it via a duplex roller chain. On the front end of the crankshaft outside of the detachable front support plate there was a high-output 12 volt alternator. The contact points for the coil ignition sat on the front end of the camshaft, with the alternator and ignition hidden behind the tall one-piece front cover. The full-flow paper-element oil filter was housed on the right just above the oil pan. The filter was held in place by a three-screw cover plate.

New alloy cylinder barrels with shrunk-in cast-iron liners were secured together with the alloy heads by four, long through-studs with an additional two, shorter extra bolts between each head-and-barrel assembly. On

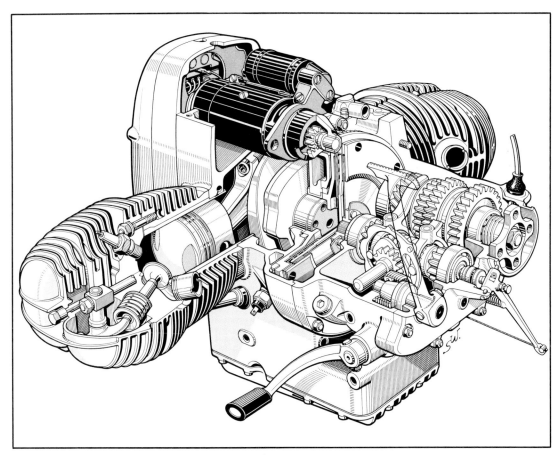

Sectioned drawing of the /5 series engine and
four-speed gearbox, with the electric starter
motor uncovered.

the outer ends of the through-studs, the
rocker supports were also bolted down to
the cylinder heads. The design of the valve
operation did not change much, but the
pushrod tubes, now mounted below the barrels acted as drains for the rocker box oil; the
oil supply was via internal lines.

All ancillary equipment on the machine
was updated. The big 24 liter or 6¼ gallon
gas tank and the flat seat, which was hinged
on the right-hand side and could be swung
open to give access to the tool tray, gave the
/5 Series a whole new appearance, along
with the new mufflers that were angled up-
wards at the rear. Plastic fenders were used
front and rear painted in the same color as
the tank and adorned with the usual twin-

line pinstriping. Four turn signal lights were
now used, and the speedometer built into
the headlamp was supplemented by a small
tachometer set into the same dial. Reminis-
cent of the old days was the typical headlamp
switch with sliding cover, which used the
same key common to all BMWs since 1954,
which in itself dated back to 1935.

The new range comprised three models,
the 500 cc R50/5, 600 cc R60/5 and a new 750
cc, the R75/5. The different engine capaci-
ties were achieved with three sizes of cylinder bore and their respective cylinder head
and valve sizes. The R50/5 had a 67 mm bore
mated to the standard 70.6 mm stroke. Its
496 cc engine produced 32 PS at 6400 rpm. A
73.5 mm bore size on the R60/5 made 599 cc

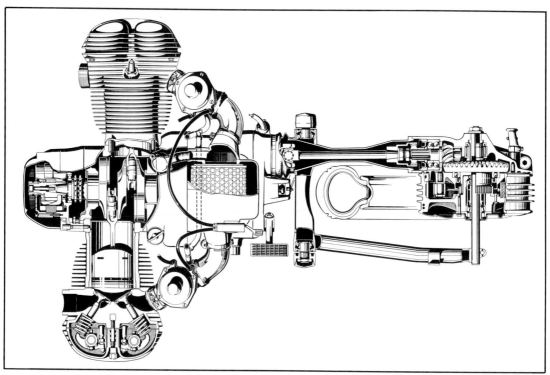

The complete R75/5 drivetrain assembly, showing plainly how offset those opposed cylinders
really were.

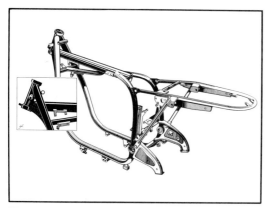

The new /5 frame with bolt-on rear subframe.
The frame was definitely not strong enough to
support the stresses of a sidecar, although
numerous firms and individuals experimented,
with varying degrees of success, with adaptor
plates and mounts for those wanting to haul a
sidecar.

and 40 PS at 6400 rpm, while the big engine
of the R75/5 had an 82 mm bore and 50 PS at
6200 rpm.

All three engines were furnished with
newly designed carburetors from Bing. The
two smaller engines shared the 26 mm
needle-jet instrument with concentric float
bowl, but for the R75/5 car-type constant
vacuum carburetors with butterfly throttle
valves were used. The CV carburetors were
big units with the characteristic dome on top
and a 32 mm choke size. Top speeds for the
three new /5 BMW models were said to be
98, 104 and 105 mph, respectively; dry
weight for all models was 418 lb. with 11 lb.
less when the optional electric starter was
not fitted to the R50/5. Prices were still considerably higher outside Germany in comparison with British or Japanese models, but
the quality was regarded to be superior on
the BMW motorcycles with engine power
and handling now much on par with the
competition. The /5 Series models were a

Year and model	1969-1973 R75/5
Engine	Overhead-valve flat twin
Bore and stroke	82x70.6 mm
Displacement	745 cc
Horsepower	50 PS at 6200 rpm
Carburetion	Twin Bing CVs, 32 mm
Ignition	Coil
Lubrication	Wet sump
Gearbox	Four-speed
Clutch	Single disc, dry
Frame	Twin tube
Suspension	Telescopic front forks; swing arm rear
Brakes	Drums, twin-leading shoe at the front
Wheels and tires	3.25x19 front; 4.00x18 rear
Wheelbase	54.5 in.; 56.5 in. 1973
Weight	419 lb. dry
Seat height	33.5 in.
Top speed	110 mph

success from the start with the US buyers taking the biggest share of annual production.

The new models had done away with the staid image of the traditional BMW touring motorcycle. They now appealed to the more sporting-oriented public as well. The sole color was no longer the deep traditional black, with the rare white exception, and the new color range was expanded year after

year. In 1972 a smaller 18 liter or 4½ gallon gas tank with chrome side panels and additional chromed covers on the rear subframe to hide the battery gave the BMW an even more flashy appearance, but this was thought to be a bit much by many buyers who opted for the unadorned big tank instead. After only one year, the chrome side covers and panels were no longer used, and the smaller tank was produced with just plain painted sides.

The first technical modification to speak of concerned the rear swing arm which was lengthened by 50 mm at the beginning of the 1973 season. This gave improved straight-line stability, but at the same time more space to fit a larger battery; there had been complaints about draining the small battery all too easily through the use of the electric starter.

Further redesign work was underway for the 1974 models, which were released in October 1973. This time BMW was not only up to date in meeting the most recent trends in the motorcycle world, but was really in the forefront in some respects. It had been rumored for quite a while that the R75/5 would not be the largest BMW for long, and that a further overbored version had been

The R50/5 with higher US type handlebars fitted. This was the only model where an electric starter was still an option. In all outward appearances the 500 cc version was identical to its larger siblings, except for the name tags on the engine cases.

The flagship of the 1971 /5 series, this R75/5 is shown with the DOT-mandated side reflectors and the high, US market handlebars, which immediately became old-fashioned when the R90S with its low Euro bars made its debut a few years later. *Vintage BMW Bulletin, Richard Kahn*

In 1972 the /5 models were available with this 18 liter or 4½ gallon gas tank, chrome panels and chrome battery covers. Seen here is an R75/5. Today, more than 20 years later, these "toaster tank" models still elicit all sorts of head shaking and criticism—while others are dedicated to the traditional styling of the bike.

The small 4½ gallon gas tank without chrome panels tells us that this is the 1973 model R75/5; the controversial chrome had lasted but one year. Again, the US models had the higher handlebars and the large, round DOT-mandated reflectors on the headlight ears and rear fender.

part of the plan from the start. The presumed R90/5, or R75S as other people were expecting, never materialized; instead, the new 1974 models included the R90/6 and R90S. The R90S was one of the first Superbikes in the sense of being a sporting motorcycle with a powerful engine and radical styling. With 67 PS on tap from the engine with its 90 mm bore, the 898 cc BMW only reached the output level of a Honda CB750 Four, but as usual with the German Boxers the basic figures on paper did not reveal the full story. The R90S was able to top 125 mph—still quite an achievement in 1973.

An absolute first for BMW was the R90S handlebar fairing, the plastic hump at the tail end of the dual seat and the smoke grey custom paint. The increased engine output was achieved by a high 9.5:1 compression ratio and 38 mm carburetors with accelerator pumps from the Italian manufacturer Dell'Orto. To handle the power a hydraulic steering damper was reintroduced that was similar to the R69S unit, which was adjusted

by the knob on the steering head. Much more important, the R90S was brought to a stop by a twin-disc front brake setup, with calipers made by ATE in Germany.

Strangely though, the R90S was outsold by the mundane R90/6 despite the worldwide popularity of the new generation of Superbikes. The touring 900 with its 60 PS engine could only be distinguished from its 750 cc counterpart by the inscriptions on the engine and the side panels, and even the Bing CV carburetors were identical. The R75/6 and the R60/6 were updated with the new five-speed gearbox and a single-disc front brake, new handlebar switches, an instrument panel with separate speedometer and tachometer, new plastic side panels and many minor refinements that were part of the steady development work typical of BMW. The 500 cc model was dropped from the range with the R60/6 now acting as the basic mount offered to fleet buyers for police forces throughout the world, which accounted for it retaining the old drum front brake.

Riding a 1969 R75/5

The new generation of BMW Boxers came exactly in time for the reawakening interest in motorcycles in Germany, with the R75/5 becoming a symbol of a change. No longer a cheap runabout, the motorcycle was now a fashionable pasttime toy. Soon after its introduction, the horsepower figures of the 750 cc BMW were surpassed by more and more models from other manufacturers, but actual performance on the road sometimes gave a different picture.

No longer was the awkward kickstart ceremony required on the R75/5, as there was an electric starter motor fitted to it, and the carburetors also had no ticklers. All that was required was the turning of the choke lever on the left of the air-filter housing and a push on the starter button on the handlebars. A crisp noise from the cylinder heads and the exhausts soon turned out a deep throaty sound and sitting down on the high dualseat and twisting the throttle brought a strong sideways move to the whole machine. On the European version, where narrow handlebars were mounted, the opposed cylinders seemed to be wider. Getting on the move brought the same lift of the rear end as before. The gearchange was a little bit improved but the "clunk," the noisiest part of the motorcycle, still remained.

That a quite a lot of development had been put into the new chassis is soon revealed by the easy steering and lightfooted handling of the physically large-appearing BMW, with an ideal riding position contributing to this good impression. The large gas tank could not be better shaped, the seat height is appreciated in its distance from the footrests, and the handlebars do not feel so narrow as soon as some speed has been achieved. Only long-legged riders will experience problems with their shins touching the carburetors and manifolds.

The 50 PS (or 57 SAE hp) can really be used on all kinds of road as soon as one gets accustomed to the up and down movement of the rear end. And with the long-travel telescopics

at the front, the nosediving under braking has to be taken into account. The twin-leading-shoe front brake was capable twenty years ago, but not too much should be expected compared to the current four-piston-caliper, twin-disc setups. Nevertheless, the 750 BMW was rated as one of the best-handling motorcycles of its time, and this is evident especially on sinuous mountain roads with no fear of grounding the cylinder head covers.

A top speed of 115 mph was no longer spectacular at the beginning of the 1970s, but there were no other contenders which could hold that sort of speed for a long time on the German autobahns. The BMW stayed oiltight, nothing vibrated loose and the rider did not get exhausted. For long-distance high-speed travel, the R75/5 set a new standard; it was not only a roadburner but an ideal mount for gentlemanly slow touring as well. It could be ridden calmly, with almost whisper quiet and without fuss. Still, top-gear acceleration was available whenever needed throughout the rpm range from the torquey engine. It also made no real difference whether there was a solo rider or a two-up couple on the BMW, for roadholding and performance did not change significantly, and on the wide rear half of the seat there was certainly room enough for a passenger. The passenger footrests were well down to avoid a cramped position, and the preload on the springs of the rear suspension could be adjusted. It took some care, however, to avoid melting the heels of one's boots on the hot, angled ends of the new mufflers.

Author Stefan Knittel rode many thousands of troublefree miles on his silver-grey R75/5 and went through only one bad time when the chassis setup was disturbed by an over-enthusiastic BMW specialist who talked him into having a hydraulic steering damper fitted instead of the standard friction one, along with stronger fork springs. This together with a different sort of rear tire took the harmony away from the handling. A standard tune, with only basic attention to the routine service jobs, is all a /5 needs and it will run forever.

While there were always improvements made from one year to another the only significant changes came in 1975 with the drilled disc brake rotors for better braking in wet weather, plus a new paint scheme for

the R90S in bright Daytona orange with red pinstriping.

After only three years the /6 Series was replaced in autumn 1976 when the 1977 range was released. The gas tank shape from

A specially equipped 1973 R75/6 for the French police with solo seat, valanced front fender, radio box, leather bags and a toolbox sunk into the top of the large gas tank. All these special-order police items can still be found today at flea markets or on dusty dealer shelves.

A little leg certainly didn't hurt, but on its introduction the R90S didn't need any help in finding eager buyers. This is the 1974 edition with undrilled front brakes, which was only available in a smoke grey or "Silver Smoke" two-tone paint scheme.

the R90S and newly designed cylinder head covers distinguished the R60/7 and R75/7 from their predecessors. A 4 mm increase in the cylinder bores to 94 mm resulted in the new 980 cc engines for the R100 models, which replaced the R90/6 and R90S. In addition to the new R100/7 and R100S there soon was to be another much applauded top-of-the-line BMW, the R100RS.

In spite of the RS designation similar to the Rennsport RS54, the R100RS was not the expected overhead-camshaft engine descendant of the competition flat twin that dominated sidecar racing for twenty years, but only a 70 PS pushrod unit. The R100RS made headline news with something completely different, as it was the first production motorcycle that came with a full fairing, which in the case of BMW was a very sporting-looking fiberglass shell. Developed after much wind-tunnel testing, the design afforded effective protection from wind and rain for the rider without the bulbous

The first Superbike from BMW was the R90S introduced in late 1973. Its styling, especially the seat and small sport fairing, created such a stir that all the other brands, from Honda to Harley-Davidson, soon imitated the R90S. This bike has the smoke grey paint scheme—quite a departure from BMW's staid image.

dimensions of other attempts in that field. In fact the R100RS resembled a racer much more than the tourer that it really was. This might have caused some misunderstanding in the beginning when the RS was not able

The Daytona orange R90S with drilled disc brakes arrived in 1975. Both it and the smoke grey version of 1973–74 became instant classics and are two of the most desirable post 1970 BMWs to be found on the used motorcycle market.

Year and model	1973–1976 R90S
Engine	Overhead-valve flat twin
Bore and stroke	90x70.6 mm
Displacement	898 cc
Horsepower	67 PS at 7000 rpm
Carburetion	Twin Dell'Ortos, 38 mm
Ignition	Coil
Lubrication	Wet sump
Gearbox	Five-speed
Clutch	Single disc, dry
Frame	Twin tube
Suspension	Telescopic front forks; swing arm rear
Brakes	Twin discs front; drum rear
Wheels and tires	3.25x19 front; 4.00x18 rear
Wheelbase	57.6 in.
Weight	452 lb. dry
Seat height	32 in.
Top speed	125 mph

Recognizing a good thing, BMW soon introduced the small R90S sport or bikini fairing on other models as optional equipment.

Another BMW first in 1975 was the drilled discs on the R90S, which improved wet weather braking performance. These drilled discs soon became available on other BMW models.

to match the top speed of the former R90S, but every long-distance rider would soon appreciate the real advantages of this model.

With their new flagship selling well, BMW had to step up motorcycle production at the Berlin factory, selling a new record of 31,515 bikes in 1977. The next new-model release had to wait until 1978. The only change during 1977 was the replacement of the R75/7 by the R80/7 with a bigger cylinder bore of 84.8 mm and a lower compression ratio to achieve the same 50 PS. This had been made in order to adapt the engine to the needs of some overseas police forces who could only get low-octane gasoline.

Realizing the demand for new smaller-capacity models to complement the BMW range, new projects were centered around the possibility of using as many components as possible from existing models and from the old /5 Series. In the end this aim was not quite realized when the R45 and R65 went into production from March 1978 on. Physically these two new small twins were not much smaller in their dimensions than their

one-liter counterparts, and the technical layout was not that much different. A shorter stroke of 61.5 mm was mated to 70 mm bores for the 473 cc R45, which was mainly intended for the 27 PS insurance class in Germany. It was available with 35 PS at

The 900 cc R90/6 differed from the 750 cc R75/6 only in the bore size and an additional 10 PS. The 1975 R90/6 produced 60 PS at 6500 rpm and accelerated to 60 mph in 5.2 seconds.

The R Series valve recession problem

At the time of the federally mandated phase-out of lead additives in gasoline in the late 1970s, BMW changed the material used in the manufacture of valve seats in anticipation of the inevitable disappearance of lead. All BMW twins built after the end of the 1980 model year were fitted with the new valve seats, with attendant problems.

The 1980–84 BMWs, which were fitted with the new composition exhaust valve seats, immediately began to experience problems in exhaust valve recession with or without the use of leaded gas, while the pre 1980 BMWs still seemed unaffected. The problems in the post 1980 BMWs were caused by bad heat-transfer characteristics, a fault of the valve seat material, and these problems may have been further exacerbated by the disappearance of lead, which had served to lubricate and cool the seat surface. The problems may have influenced BMW's decision to halt the importation of the R100 series in 1984, while the less-stressed R80 models, with less severe problems, still remained available.

By 1988, a new exhaust valve seat made of special tool steel was introduced, which seems to have solved all prior problems. As of the summer of 1990, these new seats are now being stocked by BMW of North America, which will also provide instructions and recommendations on their use in retrofitting.

Unfortunately, those 1970–79 BMWs of the /5 through /7 Series, previously considered immune to the heat transfer and expected recession problem which afflicted the post 1980 models, are now all falling victim to the same malaise, an illness delayed only by the residual lead remaining in the cylinder heads. The first symptoms are a poor idle, and an inability to correct the idle problem in spite of tuning and valve adjustments.

When contemplating the purchase of a 1970–79 BMW, pay close attention to the idle; when considering a 1980–84 twin, ask if the valve seats have recently been replaced with the new, proper seats. In most cases, these models will all have many thousands of miles on the clock and will probably be ready for some top-end attention anyway, so don't let the specter of exhaust valve seat lash closure scare you away. Now that BMW has addressed the cause, and now that the newest valve seats are available, it should be a simple matter to cure the problem once and for all.

The 1973–74 R60/6 retained the old drum front brake, but had the new five-speed gearbox, new seat and the new separate instrument cluster like its larger siblings. The gas tank still held 18 liters or 4½ gallons. The R60/6 produced 40 PS at 6400 rpm.

The first /6 models did not have a decorative decal indicating engine capacity on the battery covers. Again, European models were blessed by not having to carry those huge, hideous US reflectors. This is a 1973–74 R60/6.

The first fully faired production motorcycle, the BMW R100RS, introduced in late 1976. The 980 cc Boxer produced 70 PS at 7250 rpm; acceleration 0–60 mph took 4.6 seconds.

The limited-production, high-performance R100RS Motorsport version, available only in pure white with a red "eyebrow" over the headlight. Today this is another highly desirable BMW. Finding an owner willing to part with one is becoming increasingly difficult.

7250 rpm everywhere else except in the United States, where it was never part of the BMW model line. The 649 cc of the R65 resulted from 82 mm bores and led to 45 PS, increased to 50 PS at 7250 rpm during 1980. The enlarged version became popular in England as it was positioned in a cheaper insurance class than the bigger models, and was attractively priced from the start. A different, more angular style for the 22 liter or 5¾ gallon gas tank was used, and the seat was mated with cast-alloy wheels. A single-disc brake was used at the front while a drum brake was incorporated in the rear wheel.

The R45 and R65 range remained largely unchanged until production ended in 1985 when the dwindling demand no longer justified the luxury of two distinct ranges of flat twins in the BMW program. For the last four years an additional model with a futuristic headlamp cowling, different seat tail end, black exhaust system and a twin-disc front brake was featured in the program as the R65LS. It did not sell too well as the cosmetic

Year and model	1976–1984 R100RS
Engine	Overhead-valve flat twin
Bore and stroke	94x70.6 mm
Displacement	980 cc
Horsepower	70 PS at 7250 rpm
Carburetion	Twin Bing CVs, 40 mm
Ignition	Coil
Lubrication	Wet sump
Gearbox	Five-speed
Clutch	Single disc, dry
Frame	Twin tube
Suspension	Telescopic front forks; swing arm rear
Brakes	Twin discs front; drum rear, rear disc from 1978 on
Wheels and tires	3.25x19 front; 4.00x18 rear
Wheelbase	57.6 in.
Weight	463 lb. dry
Seat height	32 in.
Top speed	122 mph

changes were not to everybody's taste of what a BMW should look like.

Cast-alloy wheels had been introduced for the bigger models in 1977, and a rear disc brake was added during the following season. With a different and much wider top half of the fairing featuring a higher windshield, a new model was introduced in 1978 as the R100RT. High-level handle bars instead of the racey clip-ons the RS wore led to a comfortable upright riding position and together with a wide accessory range this was primarily aimed at the US market where luxury tourers were becoming more and more popular. The basic R100/7 was renamed the R100T with 65 instead of 60 PS as before. An additional 5 PS transformed the R100S into the 70 PS R100CS.

All 980 cc engines were fed by 40 mm Bing CV carburetors. Further modifications came in 1981 with brake calipers from the Italian firm Brembo, Galnikal-plated cylinder bores for less wear, a deeper alloy oil pan under the crankcase and a larger intake air filter in a new black box on top of the gearbox. Improvements to the gearbox, especially in the ease of changing the gears, led to a repositioned gear lever and a short outside linkage.

It had been a long time since BMW was actively involved in international motorcycle sports events and the roaring flat twins were even missing from the International Six Days Trials. In the ISDT a special kind of

The wind-tunnel-developed, all-enveloping full fairing on the R100RS looked like a racing fairing, provided excellent weather protection and still allowed a top speed of nearly 125 mph. It too was soon copied by many other motorcycle manufacturers.

After a few early examples with wire wheels, the R100RS rolled on these cast-alloy wheels for 1977. The wheels were cast to look like spoked wheels.

motorcycle had evolved over the years as mostly lightweight two-strokes, even in the larger-capacity classes. For the commercial motorcycle market, however, development had run in a different direction, with big four-strokes being preferred. This was also the case with the enduro models, motorcycles that looked like trials machines but were used primarily on the road. BMW therefore took keener interest, and reentered the ISDT scene in 1979 with specially developed motorcycles for a team of factory riders. The intention to follow these with a more civilized version for the enduro market was obvious enough.

The R80G/S was first shown in September 1980 and was based on the road model, but with a 21 in. wheel and high-level fender at the front and an all new single-sided swing-arm suspension at the rear. The exhaust system fed into a big muffler on the left-hand side, mounted above the rear wheel. A white gas tank and a bright red seat made for a striking contrast with the familiar BMW

The unadorned 980 cc R100/7 was a pleasant tourer and could still reach 110 mph, even without benefit of a fairing. Power was 60PS at 6500 rpm.

styling scheme, but then so did the whole machine. Critics who feared that it was far too heavy for an off-road model were right, but the buying public quickly discovered its other qualities. First, the R80G/S, with its high ground clearance, revised chassis geometry and less weight compared to the BMW road models, handled so effortlessly and nimbly on even the most twisty road that it was soon preferred over the standard R80. It then proved to be a most enduring mount for adventurous journeys to far-flung places like the Sahara Desert or Baja Peninsula. In 1984 a huge 32 liter or $8\frac{1}{3}$ gallon gas tank together with a single seat and a large luggage grid mounted behind it became available as a Paris-Dakar version, not truly

A larger-capacity R80/7 supplanted the R75/7 during 1977. Power was now down to 55 PS—50 PS on low-grade gas.

Despite an additional 82 cc, the R100S lost 2 PS over the old R90S. This was due to the new Bing CV carburetors as opposed to the former's Dell-

Ortos. The R100S, however, heralded the reappearance of the already classic R90S fairing.

New handlebar switches had been introduced by 1975, but the sunk-in filler cap, seen first on the R100RS, was new for the /7 series. The switch contacts were now silver-plated.

An R100/7 festooned with just some of the many BMW-distributed touring accessories available at the time: high-rise windscreen, additional foglamp and high-beam headlamp, high-rise handlebars and large, sturdy side luggage boxes.

To allow the relaxed upright riding position favored in the United States, a new fairing top half was designed for the R100RT. This is the first 1978 duo-tone paint version, quite striking in blue and silver.

intended for the desert endurance race, but for the adventurous long-distance traveller.

A short-lived model released in 1982 and based on the R80G/S was the R80ST with a 19 in. front wheel, low fender, road tires and less spectacular colors. Its styling, midway between enduro and roadster, was never really accepted, so the ST was dropped from the range after two years. Nobody could have foreseen the fashion tastes of six years later, when the scrambler design was in much demand, especially in France and Italy.

The other new R80 in 1982 was the R80RT. As a less-expensive edition of the R100RT with the same touring fairing, it was based on the standard R80/7 and not on the enduro chassis.

In 1983 the BMW Boxers celebrated their sixtieth anniversary, but the motorcycling world turned its attention to the Munich company in the eager anticipation of a new chapter in BMW history, the much-rumored

The proud French Motorway Patrol gendarmes got efficient RS fairings for their 1977 R80/7 models, plus the valanced front fender, which helped keep the rider dry.

Year and model	1984-on R80
Engine	Overhead-valve flat twin
Bore and stroke	84x70.6 mm
Displacement	798 cc
Horsepower	50 PS at 6500 rpm
Carburetion	Twin Bing CVs, 32 mm
Ignition	Electronic
Lubrication	Wet sump
Gearbox	Five-speed
Clutch	Single disc, dry
Frame	Twin tube
Suspension	Telescopic front forks; single-sided rear swing arm
Brakes	Disc front; drum rear
Wheels and tires	90/90x18 front; 120/90x18 rear
Wheelbase	56.7 in.
Weight	463 lb.
Seat height	31.7 in.
Top speed	115 mph

K Series. It was not until the autumn of 1983 that the new four-cylinder models were first shown to the press, to become available soon thereafter. The Boxers meanwhile still did well enough in the sales figures, but their future seemed uncertain.

At the International Motorcycle Show in Cologne in September 1984 a clear statement was made and the new R80 road models showed the direction BMW was to go in the future. A modified monolever rear swing arm, new front forks and wheels similar to the K Series and slight design changes for the R80 and R80RT together with a more effective exhaust system brought the two models up to date. The R80G/S enduro was

A new middleweight BMW was introduced in 1978 with the 473 cc R 45. Power was 35 bhp.

Unfortunately, the R45 was never available in the US market.

The ultra-short-stroke 650 cc R65 supplanted the old R60/7 in 1978. Annoying engine vibration at the new US legal top speed of 55 mph plagued the early models, something the engineers in Munich had not planned on. Simply exceeding the speed limit by a few mph solved the problem. Power was 45 bhp.

The R65LS was introduced in 1981 with styling by Hans A. Muth. The design foreshadowed the Suzuki Katana series, which Muth created as well. The LS models are quite sought after today among American enthusiasts.

The updated 1981 /7 models had a new black airbox with a larger air filter inside and Italian Brembo brake calipers instead of the former German ATE products. The R100/7 was now simply called the R100.

From 1981 on, the R100CS had the same 70 bhp engine, like the RS and RT models, and could reach 125 mph even without a full fairing. The CS model is extremely desirable and difficult to find in the United States today.

The rear disc brake on the R100RS was introduced in 1978. Shown here is a 1981 model.

shown in a new paint finish, and remained in the program as before. Production of the R45, R65 and the R100 range was stopped, with a new R65 for the German 27 PS class planned for 1985. Its only difference from the new R80 would be its short-stroke 649 cc engine with smaller valves and carburetors to detune the performance.

As it was really no problem at all to convert the R80 engine to 980 cc using barrels and heads from the factory BMW spare parts stocks, the factory management reversed their original intention to stick to the 800 cc limit for their flat twins. Dubbed a limited edition at first, the new versions of the R100RS and the R100RT were back in production in 1986 and 1987, respectively. Based on the R80, they now used the R80's single-sided rear-swing-arm suspension and the same wheels, tanks and seats; the only visible differences were the fairings and the twin-disc front brake. Yet these were no longer the powerful 980 cc models of before,

The 1981 R100RS produced 70 bhp and weighed 463 lb. Top speed was still 125 mph.

The first production enduro model from BMW was the R80G/S in 1980, with a top speed of 104 mph. Bodywork was white with the blue and red Motorsport panel on the gas tank.

The blue version of the R80G/S lacked the gaudy lobster-red seat.

The Paris-Dakar R80G/S model with its big tank was available from 1984 on to celebrate BMW's success in the famous desert endurance race. The technical specifications remained un-changed from the 1980 R80G/S. The distinctive 32 liter or 8⅓ gallon gas tank, seat, luggage rack and attendant decals are still available separately as retrofit items for the earlier models.

as new, more strict noise and emission control laws could not have been met with such a big air-cooled twin in its earlier state of tune. Consequently, low-compression pistons and the same small 32 mm carburetors as on the R80 together with the large expansion chamber on the exhaust system situated under the gearbox only allowed for 60 PS at 6500 rpm, but noise and pollution regulations were satisfied.

With the enduro models gaining in sales everywhere, more large-capacity engines soon found their way into the off-road frames. It had been long expected, therefore, for BMW to underline its leading position with a still larger enduro model. When the R100GS was at last released, it turned out not to be just an uprated model, but a whole new design. With its long-travel front forks

from the Italian specialist Marzocchi, a windshield over the headlamp, the big 26 liter or 6¾ gallon gas tank and a stepped seat, it looked much more businesslike than before. And with the single-sided Paralever swing arm at the rear with two universal joints in the driveline and the parallel torque arm anchored to the frame, the rear-end lift reaction from the shaft drive was counteracted.

A lot of detail work was spent on the engine, so that the reintroduction of the 40 mm Bing carburetors and a carefully calculated exhaust system volume resulted in new power characteristics. Output remained at 60 PS, but there was a considerable increase in the torque at low revs, which led many of the early press testers to doubt the official figures. Not surprisingly, the

A slightly modified street version of the R80G/S enduro was the R80ST from 1984. Like all the other BMW twins, the R80ST now lacked the kickstarter of the earlier models.

The updated R100RT as it was available between 1981 and 1984, in solid colors.

Single-sided swing arm, wheels and forks from the K Series bikes appeared on the new R80 twin of 1984.

In line with previous marketing successes, the new R80 was soon offered in this RT configuration, first seen in 1984. The fairing was similar in style to the R100RT.

Back by popular demand: the new R100RS was based on the 1984 model R80. The new R100RS was available in a limited edition of only 1,000 units in the first year. The new RS could run on unleaded gas.

R100GS became the best-selling BMW in Germany after its debut in 1988.

As of 1990, the BMW flat twin in its present form is alive and healthy, and sells well enough to many happy customers, but it is no longer a secret that the days of the air-cooled pushrod Boxer are running out. The only thing that is certain for the future is that BMW will never stop producing the flat twin, but it will probably look much different in the years to come.

Prospects

It is no easy task to give detailed advice to the buyer of a BMW Boxer from the last twenty years as more than 400,000 of more than thirty different models have left the Berlin factory during that period of time. Still, there are two main aspects to look into.

From the collector's point of view the essential aim would be to find or to attain in restoration an example as close as possible to original factory specification. This in most cases is not a problem, as BMW can still supply almost anything back to the early /5 models, but replacing modified parts like exhaust systems, gas tanks or fairings is expensive. With a bit of searching and the necessary luck, low-mileage examples in good original condition can still be found. The situation may be different for some models in some parts of the world, such as the R50/5, which was never sold in great numbers in the United States. A difficult problem for the restorer seeking to recapture originality is the interchangeability of parts, which have led to many upgrades, such as when footrest rubbers or mufflers needed replacing and were substituted by later parts that fit without trouble. A good idea would be to consult as many period magazine articles as one can lay one's hands

The 1000 cc R100GS from 1988 included many new technical features, such as the parallelogram swing arm called the Paralever, which encompassed the driveshaft.

on. Books, catalogs, old advertisements and official BMW owner's manuals will help as well.

When acquiring parts through an unauthorized BMW dealer it is important to know exactly what is needed, because here again, people will tend to tell you it is right and it fits anyway, which won't do anything for you if it is from the later model. What has to be avoided from the collector's point of view is aftermarket accessories from sources other than the factory stock of equipment, especially poor-quality goods coming in from the Orient.

Ratings

Until a few years ago not many people would have considered any BMW model produced after the end of the classic period, which ended with the last Earles-fork machines, as collector items. The situation has now changed. More than twenty years have

passed since the debut of the /5 Series, and their ancestry can still be seen in today's Boxers, in spite of having gone through quite a number of changes. As always, some people have had more foresight than the rest, and they kept their old R75/5 long before the term classic was applied to it. At the beginning of the 1990s, however, there is no doubt that this model, plus the R50/5 and R60/5, must rate as genuine four-star collector bikes. The 1969 to 1971 models are the ones to prefer with the 1972–73 chrome updating not quite as popular.

As the precursor of the modern Superbike, the R90S is destined to become a collectible motorcycle—and will certainly be a joy to ride in the meantime. Many of the R90S bikes seem to have fallen victim to some sort of performance modifications and updating of engine components. If you are looking for a stock bike, this will be a mark against it. On the other hand, if you are looking for a sports bike, the modifications could be a plus depending on what they are and how they have been done. Definitely a four-star motorcycle.

As for all of the other Boxers, it is too early to give any star ratings from a collector's point of view. These are bikes that are often still in everyday use and chances are, that is what most buyers will be looking for; thus, a different set of standards must be used in rating these. Most of these Boxers are worth a minimum of three stars.

The most popular and interesting models have been the first and second series R100RS and R100RT, the R80G/S and the later GS series. The rare limited-edition R100RS Motorsport and the Paris-Dakar edition R80G/S stand out among the others. Only 200 of the special Motorsport version R100RS, with its white bodywork with red and blue pinstriping, were imported into the United States, making them quite rare.

Looking to the future, it seems possible that some models which did not reach high production figures would be the next best ones to look for, such as the R65LS and the R80ST. The practical value is still more important and therefore a fully faired tourer that has been around for fourteen years and a common sight everywhere might be more attractive than a rare middleweight sporting model.

Model	Years	Type	Rating
K100	1983-on	1000 cc dohc	★★★
K100RS	1983-on	1000 cc dohc	★★★
K100RT	1984-on	1000 cc dohc	★★★
K100LT	1986-on	1000 cc dohc	★★★
K75C	1985-on	750 cc dohc	★★★
K75	1986-on	750 cc dohc	★★★
K75S	1986-on	750 cc dohc	★★★
K1	1989-on	1000 cc dohc	★★★★

K Series 1983-On

Exactly sixty years after the first BMW was shown to the public at the Paris Motorshow in October 1923, a completely new BMW motorcycle design made its debut at the same venue. The long development in search of both more power and a still unmistakable BMW image led to the adoption of an in-line four-cylinder configuration. The liquid-cooled engine was set longitudinally into the chassis, keeping the driveline with the gearbox behind and the shaft to the rear wheel—a look back to BMW's motorcycling tradition. In addition the engine was inclined 90 degrees to the left. This setup was christened by the marketing people as the BMW Compact Drive System and was hailed as a unique design.

The project had been started in spring 1978 under the heading K and when it was ready five and a half years later, the production model was called the K100 to indicate the capacity of nearly 1000 cc. Bore and stroke were set at an undersquare 67x70 mm to shorten the total length of the engine unit. The plated cylinder bores were part of the one-piece crankcase casting into which the crankshaft was set from the right-hand side and the oil pan bolted to the bottom. A timing chain ran up at the front end to the twin overhead camshafts which opened two valves per cylinder via bucket-type cam followers. Fed by Bosch electronic fuel injection, the mixture was ignited by a digital

control system; with a compression ratio of 10.2:1, power was 90 PS at 8000 rpm.

Because the inclined engine had to be centered in the frame it was not possible to take the drive directly from the crankshaft; a secondary shaft driven from a set of spur gears and mounted below the crankshaft took the drive to the single-disc dry clutch, which in turn drove the five-speed gearbox. The single-sided swing arm was cast in alloy and contained the driveshaft, which was bolted together with the rear-wheel-drive housing. The massive engine-transmission unit was suspended from a lightweight frame built from short lengths of straight tubing. Four bolts were enough to join the components, while a fifth one held the rear suspension strut to the frame with the swing arm mounted to the gearbox case.

The basic model had a totally redesigned gas tank, seat, side panels and headlamp cowling, but the centerpiece clearly was the huge engine block with the airbox set above it. As an important part of the design package, the radiator received a fairing with the typical front grille shape seen in the BMW cars.

The top-of-the-line model, the K100RS, became available with a narrow and distinctively styled fairing that was soon regarded as a masterpiece in combining individual appearance with effective protection from the

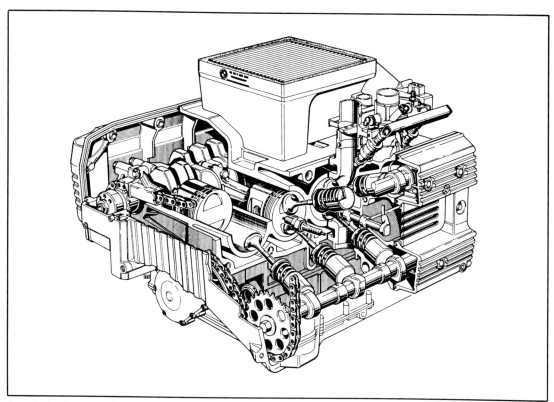

A technical tour de force—and a break with over 60 years of flat-twin tradition—the BMW K Series engine. After numerous other designs were investigated and eventually discarded, BMW astounded the motorcycle world with the K100 and its four-cylinder engine, inclined by 90 degrees, which was water cooled and fitted with twin overhead camshafts. To many, it looked like a small car engine lying on its side.

Called the BMW Compact Drive System, the rear swing arm was mounted to the gearbox and the whole assembly put into the frame as a unit, becoming a major structural member.

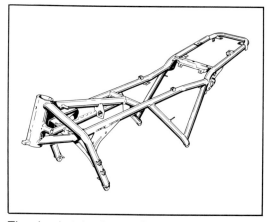

The simple tube-frame of the BMW K Series.

elements. A much bulkier fairing was used on the K100RT, which soon completed the range. As with the respective Boxer models, the RS was the sports tourer while the RT provided an upright and more relaxed position for the touring rider.

The list of new details on the K 100 series is long, from a four-into-one exhaust system made in stainless steel, to the 22 liter or 5¾ gallon aluminum gas tank with built-in fuel pump, to the specially developed handlebar switches. Success could not have been better for BMW, with the initial sales justifying the enormous development effort and the costly technical equipment, which turned the Berlin factory into one of the most advanced of its kind. In 1985 more than 37,000 BMW motorcycles were produced there, an all-time record, especially when measured against today's declining motorcycle sales.

The K75 made its appearance in 1985 as a three-cylinder version of the K100. The three-cylinder 740 cc engine had the crankpins spread at 120 degrees and the secondary shaft gained two counterweights at its ends to counterbalance the inherent vibration of the engine configuration. The front downtubes of the frame had to be reangled to compensate for the shorter engine. Furnished with a small handlebar fairing and a drum-braked 18 in. rear wheel, the K75C was the first model available. It was followed the next year by the K75S with the 17 in. wheel and disc brake from the K100, but its most distinguishing feature was the sporting short fairing with a small tinted screen and turn signals at the upper edges.

Higher-domed pistons in the K75 increased the compression ratio to 11.0:1 and with 75 PS at 8500 rpm, the relative output of the smaller engine was superior to that of the K100. Less weight, between 20 and 40 lb. depending on the model, and a generally smoother engine which provided more bottom-end torque, made choosing between the K75 and the K100 a tough choice.

Additions to both ends of the K Series were made in 1986 with the basic K75 at one end of the price list and the fully equipped K100LT at the other. The K100LT was a luxury tourer with colour-matched luggage side cases and a top box with a passenger

The basic unfaired K100 model, seen here in pre-production 1983 form. The design and styling of the K Series in some ways polarized BMW enthusiasts, with some traditionalists remaining loyal to the older Boxer design, while many embraced the progress, born of necessity, that the K Series represented. In spite of the controversy, most manage to justify owning at least one of each type, and many new K bike owners long to own a pre 1970 as well.

backrest attached to it, a deeply padded seat and a cassette-radio all included in the standard package with many other options. The opposite path was taken by the K75, which came with no fairing at all and a chromed headlamp instead, polished fork sliders and heat shield on the silencer, an orange-coloured double pinstripe (the first pinstriping on a K bike) over black bodywork, and to top it all a bright orange seat.

BMW was the first in the motorcycle world when it introduced the ABS anti-locking brake system for the K100 in 1987. As of 1990, the K100 with ABS has not seen any competition from the Japanese giants.

Competition with, and success over, the Japanese Superbike designs was BMWs main goal, and this was to be achieved in 1989 with an uprated K bike, the futuristically

The new K100RS, with its wind-tunnel-developed fairing, which eliminated virtually all wind buffetting, and did much to aid straight-line stability at high speeds. Power was 90 PS.

A car-type headlight, twin signals built into the mirror bodies and an adjustable spoiler on top of the screen completed the radical new look of the K100RS.

The cockpit view of the K100RS, probably the most extensive instrument panel on any modern production motorcycle.

A limited-edition K100RS from 1987 with all-black RS Style design, which again was soon to be copied by BMW's Japanese competitors.

styled K1. The K1 engine received a four-valve cylinder head and a new central computerized fuel injection and ignition setup to make a full 100 PS available. The latest large disc brakes with four-piston calipers and the Paralever design of the rear swing arm with two joints and a torque tube were used. A huge fairing and front fender set the style for the K1 with blue or red bodywork and avant garde graphics.

Customers who preferred the conservative BMW look to the striking K1 could choose the K100RS when it inherited the same technical specification for the 1990 model year.

Year and model	1983–1989 K100RS
Engine	In-line four cylinder, double overhead camshafts
Bore and stroke	67x70 mm
Displacement	987 cc
Horsepower	90 PS at 8000 rpm
Carburetion	Bosch electronic fuel injection
Ignition	Digital electronic
Lubrication	Wet sump
Gearbox	Five-speed
Clutch	Single disc, dry
Frame	Tubular space frame
Suspension	Telescopic front forks; single-sided rear swing arm
Brakes	Twin discs front; single disc rear
Wheels and tires	100/90x18 front; 130/90x17 rear
Wheelbase	59.5 in.
Weight	557 lb.
Seat height	32 in.
Top speed	137 mph

Prospects

There are not too many things a prospective K Series motorcycle buyer must be warned about. On average the machines seem to be used much more than most other motorcycles for running up thousands of miles on their speedometers—and not without reason, as almost no serious complaints have been noticed over the last seven years. This also presents a considerably lower risk

A bigger fairing top half and the high windscreen were features of the long-distance-tourer K100RT. Everything on the motorcycle, including the riders' helmets and leathers, came from the newly developed BMW Accessory Program.

when choosing a high-mileage example as an affordable secondhand buy.

Sometimes the number of miles on the clock will be mirrored in the finish of the machine with scratches on the plastic components and traces of wear on the hard-to-

The 1987 K100LT came with a different windscreen on the fairing, molded seat cover and luggage cases as well as a top box with backrest—all standard equipment.

The K100LT cockpit with optional cassette player and additional instruments, items mostly favored by the American buyer.

clean rough casting surfaces, but that does not necessarily denote worn-out mechanical components. It really depends on the money one has available to spend, as there are many good examples around everywhere, with the total production having passed the 100,000 mark as of 1990.

The only serious complaint with K Series bikes has been of high-speed vibration and of oil leaking into the cylinder when the

Year and model	1986-on K75
Engine	In-line three cylinder, double overhead camshafts
Bore and stroke	67x70 mm
Displacement	740 cc
Horsepower	75 PS at 8500 rpm
Carburetion	Bosch electronic fuel injection
Ignition	Digital electronic
Lubrication	Wet sump
Gearbox	Five-speed
Clutch	Single disc, dry
Frame	Tubular space frame
Suspension	Telescopic front forks; single-sided rear swing arm
Brakes	Twin discs front; drum rear
Wheels and tires	100/90x18 front; 120/90x18 rear
Wheelbase	59.5 in.
Weight	502 lb.
Seat height	32 in., 29 in. optional
Top speed	122 mph

A three-cylinder version was added to the BMW range in 1985. This is the K75C with its small handlebar fairing. Power was 75 PS.

The K75S, introduced for sale in the United States in the summer of 1986, came with a narrow half fairing and lower engine shrouds. Reduced suspension travel gave sportier, if somewhat controversial, handling qualities.

An unfaired K75 was added in 1987, painted black with an orange-red seat and pinstriping.

Riding a 1985 K100RS

BMW could easily have developed an up-to-date high-performance motorcycle. Powerful four-cylinder engines are nothing new to the Munich R&D staff—and didn't the most powerful four to date come from BMW in the shape of the 1.5 liter turbo engine that won the automobile Formula 1 World Championship in 1983? It was a four-cylinder BMW motorcycle that made its debut at about the same time, but it was not intended to provide such maximum output. Still, it was part of a totally new concept for BMW motorcycles.

The targets were reached, the K Series BMWs became a major attraction for both the press and the buying public all over the world, and they still are. Buying a new one is out of the question for a lot of people if only for financial reasons, but an increasing number can now be found on the secondhand market. So what makes them so desirable?

Not only is the technical concept, with the inclined longitudinal engine, unique, the same is true for the design of the fairing, giving the K100RS an unmistakable appearance.

A ride starts with the standard procedure. The electronic fuel injection and ignition system still has a mechanical choke device for easy starting from cold and increased idle speed. Muted by the big stainless steel muffler, the engine does not really sound like a motorcycle unit especially since there is a high-pitched gear whine from the primary reduction gears which overrides it. After sitting down on the BMW, the peculiar colourful switches on the clip-on handlebars stand out. These have been much criticized by testers who are more used to Japanese bikes, but there is nothing truly wrong with them. Using the left thumb for the left-hand turn signals and right thumb for the right is only logical, isn't it?

From a 1000 rpm idle, the K100RS can be moved off without fuss. The engine pulls effortless like a turbine, especially considering the sound it makes, and with light action on the gear lever, one goes through the gearbox to reach top gear in no time. There is such a spread of torque that you feel as though you could even start off in fifth gear!

Unfortunately an in-line four-cylinder can't avoid some sort of vibration somewhere in the rev range; the K100RS is remarkably smooth, but there is still a short nervous period around 60 mph in fifth gear, and this is the sort of speed that is driven most of the time on an open road. There are two easy solutions: you either go slower or faster.

The small fairing takes away the feeling of speed almost completely. It is so effective in diverting the wind pressure away from the rider and the rain that the K100RS can be used like a tourer but without the need for huge bodywork. The attached mirror-cum-turn-signal bulges and the little deflector on the top end of the narrow fairing screen are well-conceived features, too.

An interesting advantage of the electronic fuel injection system is the cut-off for fuel and spark as soon as the twistgrip is closed. It not only gives a lower fuel consumption figure but it also slows down the bike through the engine's own braking effects and the three disc brakes are not required in many situations. It also helps under hard braking to use the engine to help slow the machine.

As could be expected from BMW, the handling qualities of the K100RS are faultless, as is the riding position. If you want to sit more upright on your motorcycle there is the RT or LT version available with a bigger fairing, but the RS is a perfect sports tourer as well, and it matters little if one model does 130 mph and the other 137 mph. If speed alone were the game, one of the road racer lookalikes from the Far East would be a far better bet.

---

bikes are left on their stands. The oil results in a smokey start up. BMW claims to have remedied these problems on the later K models.

Ratings

It is much too early to give any ratings on the K Series as it is a matter of personal tastes and preferences.

The most popular model by a large margin is the K100RS. The K75 Series in general seems to live in the shadow of the four-cylinder models, a fate it does not deserve. Nevertheless decide for yourself, and go for at least one test ride to find out which model suits best.

There is an endless list of options both from the new-model program and due to the

The top-of-the-line Superbike K1 appeared in 1989 with striking bodywork and an innovative styling scheme, which some critics disliked. The bike included ABS anti-lock braking and BMW's Paralever one-sided rear swing arm. Initially, the K1 was available in blue or red bodywork, both with yellow accents.

A new-look K100 with lowered seat and high-rise handlebars was available between 1987 and 1989.

interchangeability of parts so that you can transform an older one into the latest model with only a change of seat and fairing. There are numerous specialists around to ask for advice, and the classifieds in BMW club magazines in the United States and elsewhere are filled with all manner of late-model BMWs in all price ranges and conditions.

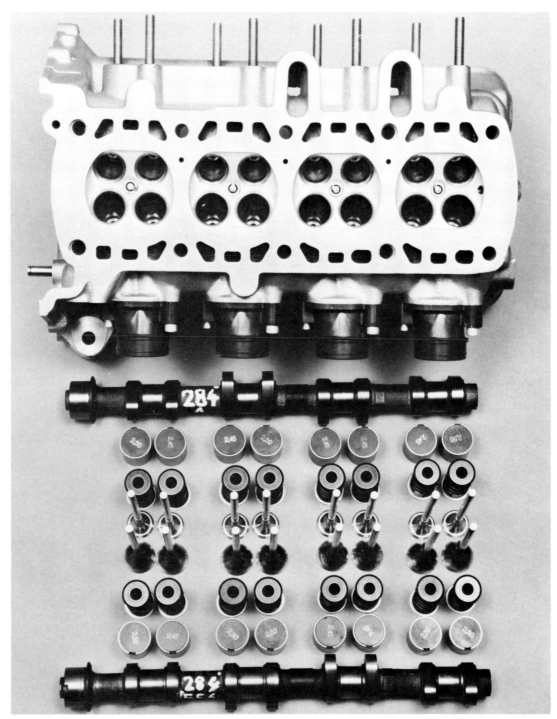

The new cylinder head for the K1 had four
valves per cylinder, which allowed the 987 cc
engine to pump out 100 PS.

Model	Year	Type	Rating
R5SS	1937	500 cc ohv	★★★★★
R51SS	1938	500 cc ohv	★★★★★
R51RS	1939	500 cc ohv	★★★★
RS54	1954	500 cc dohc	★★★★★

Production Racers 1937–1954

When BMW entered the motorcycle world in the early 1920s, racing success was seen to be the best way of advertising the virtues of a new model. It didn't matter if it was a touring model that was being touted, winning a road race was widely regarded as a sign of proven technical superiority. To achieve this, a more elaborate engine than the low-powered side-valve flat twin from the R32 was developed at the Munich factory, and it immediately justified the effort and expense with success from the first outing on. The 500 cc overhead-valve BMW firmly established the company's position at the forefront of the German motorcycle industry with an unbroken string of wins and national championships during the following years. Response from private riders

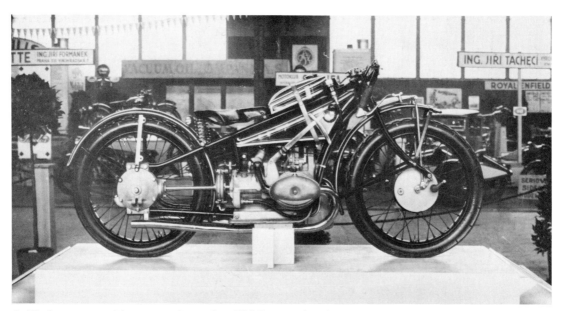

A *Werksrennmaschine* or works racing BMW shown at the 1929 Prague motorcycle exhibition. Horsepower figures in those days were closely guarded secrets, and although factory racers had production-machine origins, few internal parts were from the original engines.

Ernst Henne in 1930 on the supercharged 750 cc world record breaker. Henne used a faired helmet and tail cone of his own design. It's not known whether they made any sort of differ- ence, but that helmet shape can be seen today, 60 years later, on the heads of endurance bicycle racers the world over. Henne's record for 1930 was 221.54 Km/h or 137.35 mph.

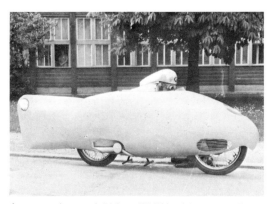

A supercharged 500cc BMW with streamlined shell ridden by factory racer Ernst Henne to establish an absolute speed record for motorcycles in 1937. The record, unbeaten for many years thereafter, was 173.5 mph.

The same record-breaker with shell partially removed, showing the outrigger wheels, which were to be lowered at the end of the run as the machine coasted to a stop, to keep it from falling on its side. Note Henne's favorite streamlined helmet.

US Vintage Club member Toby Rosner and his 1936 R5 at Langhorne, Pennsylvania, in 1939. This particular R5, a 500 cc twin of 24 PS, has had its front fender removed and front brake disconnected, a common practice when racing on dirt or cinder tracks. Rosner today still rides a similar 1953 R68 on weekends to the Rock Store near his home in California. *Vintage BMW Bulletin, Toby Rosner*

was met by a small-scale production of the R37 with the ohv engine. It was, however, not sold purely as a racing model, and it rendered the same reliable service as a modern sports roadster alongside the side-valve tourer.

Following the R37, the development of the ohv road models and the works racers no longer ran on a parallel course, with the racers still based on the tube-framed R37 at a time when the pressed-steel frames had long taken over the production models. Technical development was not taken in big steps, as it was soon realized that it would be much too expensive to attempt to rival the established British teams. Nevertheless, another field of

competition was entered, which resulted in instant success—speed record runs. With a supercharger mounted on top of the gearbox of the 750 cc pushrod engine, enough power became available to achieve a new world speed record of 135 mph in October 1929. Ernst Henne and the supercharged BMW Boxer became the main contenders for motorcycle speed records over the next eight years. His last record of 174 mph was set in 1937 and could not be bettered until 1951!

Supercharging was also applied to the road-race engines for the works riders, only to reveal the limitations of the old engine and frame designs. A radical step forward was needed and with the necessary funds now available in the mid 1930s, a racing model was conceived that appeared on the outside quite similar to the new R5 road model of 1936. Inside, the racing engine not only had a supercharger mounted to the front cover driven by the front end of the crankshaft, but two overhead camshafts were under the valve covers and a shaft and bevel drive lay on top of each cylinder. It was to become the Grand Prix winner BMW always wanted, with fearless Bavarian policeman Georg Meier becoming European Champion in 1938. He finally fulfilled his ambition in the following year, when he was the first foreign rider to win the Senior Tourist Trophy on the Isle of Man—and on a foreign machine built by BMW!

BMW could not be persuaded to build a small run of production racers for sale to private entrants, however, and it was clearly out of the question to assemble any of the dohc engines for use outside of the factory team. But something had to be done in order to support talented young riders in their competition careers, and therefore in 1937 the R5SS was prepared. Based on the standard R5, the Supersport had no lights or mufflers, and outside levers supplanted the inverted ones on the handlebars. With different valve timing together with carburetor velocity stacks and different carburetor jetting, the power output was raised to between 28 and 30 PS from the original 24. The 100 mph model, however, was never really offered to the general public, as the

Schorsch Meier on his way to winning the 1939 Isle of Man Senior Tourist Trophy. In what is perhaps the most famous BMW racing photo of all time, the winning supercharged 500 cc BMW is seen reeling off the miles, with Meier about to become the first foreigner to win the Isle of Man Tourist Trophy.

Priceless they may be, but supercharged BMWs are still being raced today. Getting envious glances from his competitors on prewar Nortons and Ariels is Walter Zeller, astride a newly restored 1939 500 cc works racer. The occasion was the 1981 Oldtimers Grand Prix at the Salzburgring in Austria. *Vintage BMW Bulletin, Dr. Helmut Krackowizer*

small batch was sold to chosen riders.

Soon after the introduction of the plunger-framed R51 road model there was another batch of racers called the R51SS assembled in 1938, but for the following season more work went into another production racer.

When introduced in 1939, the new R51RS in fact looked like the works racer with larger-diameter wheels of 21 in. at the front, 20 in. at the rear, and the same gas tank and seat. The brakes were only beefed up by stiffening rings as full-width brakes were not fitted. Still a pushrod design, the engine nevertheless showed considerable deviation from the standard R51 design with the two camshafts in the crankcase driven by spur gears instead of the long timing chain; the cylinder barrels had different fins, as on the R66. The power output had been increased

to 36 PS and allowed a top speed of 115 mph. Only twenty of the R51RS motorcycles were built and sold to preregistered customers close to the factory.

Following World War II, there were a lot of home-tuned BMW specials entered in German races. These pushrod models earned numerous good placings behind the works models and against more exotic British machinery. With an international racing ban on the use of superchargers, the factory began development of a new racer. Nevertheless the basic prewar design was retained, although numerous details were changed leading to a much smaller-looking engine. Based on the 1953 works racers with swing-arm front and rear suspension, the new production racer was announced for the coming season. Named the RS54, with RS standing for racing in German, the bevel-driven

Only 24 of the RS54 production racers were built in 1954 for private riders. Notable features of this overhead-cam 500 cc racer were the swing-arm rear suspension and Earles-pattern leading-link front forks, which appeared with only minor changes in the production R50 and R69 the following year.

An original factory photograph of the RS54 as it was delivered during 1954 with tachometer, alloy rims, alloy racing gas tank and the 500 cc overhead-cam engine.

This is the last development of the works racer as used by Walter Zeller, Geoff Duke and Dickie Dale from 1957 to 1959. The factory 498 cc engine was based on a bore and stroke of 70x64 mm, while the production racer RS54 had a 66x72 mm bore and stroke; the road model R51/3 of 1951–54 had the square 68 mm dimensions.

Year and model 1954 RS54
Engine ...... Flat-twin with bevel-driven double overhead
  camshafts
Bore and stroke .... 66x72 mm
Displacement .... 492 cc
Horsepower .... 45 PS at 8000 rpm
Carburetion .... Twin Fischer-Amals, 30 mm
Ignition .... Bosch magneto
Lubrication .... Wet sump
Gearbox .... Four-speed
Clutch .... Single disc, dry
Frame .... Twin tube
Suspension .... Swing arm front and rear
Brakes .... Drums, twin-leading shoe at the front
Wheels and tires .... 3.25x19 front; 3.50x19 rear
Weight .... 291 lb. dry
Seat height .... NA
Top speed .... 125 mph

dohc engine was finally available to private customers. Again, all of the twenty solo motorcycles and four sidecar outfits were already sold before assembly started. The main reason for such a restrictive policy was the high costs of the venture that virtually ruled out any further production.

On an international level the new top BMW rider, Walter Zeller, worked hard to keep pace with leading factory riders from England and Italy, and his machine benefited from constant development, sometimes using fuel injection in place of carburetors. The best results came at the end of the 1956 season, with Zeller finishing in second position in the 500 cc World Championship.

One of BMW's most successful riders was Walter Zeller, who became the German national champion in 1951, 1954 and 1956 and co-world champion in 1956. He is seen here in the mid 1950s on a factory 500 cc Rennsport.

The same BMW RS engine, however, set new standards in the sidecar class where it soon proved to be the ideal power unit for these outfits, especially once the outfits began to be built lower and lower to the ground. BMW factory teams won no less than eighteen individual World Championships and twenty constructor's titles between 1954 and 1974.

After the factory's road racing effort had come to an end on a Grand Prix level in 1974, several attempts were made with tuned production-based models in long-distance races or production class events, but mostly the activities were confined to private team efforts.

A full-blooded factory entry was made in cross-country racing for 1979 with the European Championship and the Interna-tional Six Days Trial, as a preliminary program prior to the launching of a production enduro model. This in turn was used as the basis for the Paris-Dakar racers that won the desert endurance event four times for BMW, in 1981, 1983, 1984 and 1985.

Prospects

Buying a BMW racer is no easy task, although it's still the dream of virtually all BMW enthusiasts the world over! The first problem will be in finding one. The second problem will be in determining whether it is a genuine racer as opposed to a mixture of dubious parts or even a replica. It is never easy to trace the history of a racing motorcycle, because it in all likelihood may have been modified from one year to another in order to keep it competitive. The best bet is always to consult as many publications as possible just to compare the pictured models to what is being offered.

There is almost no chance that a BMW works racer will turn up from an unexpected

Walter Zeller still hard at it, here in his fifties and back in the saddle of a production racer RS54 at the Oldtimer Grand Prix at the Salzburgring in Austria in 1977. *Vintage BMW Bulletin, Dr. Helmut Krackowizer*

A production racer RS54 being campaigned in the United States in the late 1950s. This racer was run by the Liebmann family of AMOL Precision fame, and used the 500 cc Rennsport motor. *Vintage BMW Bulletin, Talbot Lovering*

What at first glance looks like an RS54 is in fact an RS54 racing chassis fitted with a pushrod R50S motor. It was again campaigned by the Liebmann family in the United States in the late 1960s. Note the extra spark plug and the spark plug wrench kept handy under the seat. *Vintage BMW Bulletin, Talbot Lovering*

A restored RS54 raced by Rupert Bauer, foreman of the BMW Motorcycle Development Department in Munich. The occasion was the Oldtimer Grand Prix of 1977, where Bauer posted the fastest lap time in the 1944–1960 Postwar class at 141.48 km/h. *Vintage BMW Bulletin, Dr. Helmut Krackowizer*

Six-times world champions Klaus Enders and Ralf Engelhard on one of the unbeatable BMW RS54-engined racing outfits. The Rennsport engines truly came into their own in sidecar competiton due to the wide powerband and high torque.

The German Fulda tire factory sponsored this RS54 BMW Rennsport sidecar rig of Willi Faust and Karl Remmert in the mid 1950s. Machines such as this can once again be seen in vintage racing events, particularly in Germany and England. *Vintage BMW Bulletin, Fulda archives*

This R69S piloted by the German rider Sebastian Nachtmann took part in the 1961 International Six Days Trials. The rare two-into-one exhaust system was an over-the-counter accessory item; occasionally a set still turns up at a flea market or in the Vintage Club magazine classifieds. *Vintage BMW Bulletin, Ulrich Schwab*

Even non-Rennsport BMWs were active as sidecar racers in the 1960s. Here at the Mosport track in Canada in 1968 was the Hungarian team of Jeno Fulop and passenger George Nagy on their R69S powered outfit. *Vintage BMW Bulletin, Richard Kahn*

The factory BMW for the International Six Days
Trial in 1979. The 871 cc engine produced 55
bhp.

BMW won the gruelling Paris-Dakar desert race four times with a factory team of riders. Here is Belgian rider Gaston Rahier at speed in the Tenere Desert on his way to winning the 1987 race.

source, but even there one cannot be absolutely sure as there is more than one replica of the 1938–39 supercharged model known to exist, each of which is touted as the TT winner! Similarly, another replica of something else could therefore always show up on the market.

With the prewar production racers, the situation is complicated, as there seems to be an amazing number of them still around. It is possible with the assistance of the BMW archive records to separate the specials from the few original ones.

The RS54 is the most difficult racer to assess as there has been a steady flow of remanufactured parts from a lot of different places with skilled machinists in the United States and Canada even building some replica, or even improved, RS engines! It seems, however, that owners or prospective buyers now really care less and less whether their model is genuine, as long as it looks correct. Still, the advice for anybody preparing to hand over a large amount of money is the same: it is better to get the information before the transaction to avoid any unpleasant surprises afterward.

Ratings

Genuine BMW production racers—such as the R5SS, R51SS, R51RS and RS54—rank among the world's most coveted. All are high in the five-star bracket.

A faithful copy of an RS54 just cannot be in the same league as a real bike, simply from the historical point of view alone. The same applies to specials where a mixture of parts has come from all sorts of other models with the destruction of their respective history. There can be important specials, nevertheless, with a well-known history attached to them, especially some racers from the 1950s, which may have survived unaltered, but rating them would have to be done on an individual basis. Nevertheless, competition machines from any period are now instant collector's pieces, especially when their appearance has not been changed since the time when they were first campaigned.

Riding the 1953 RS54

The legendary BMW RS54 production racer from the 1950s is a world apart from the mature and sedate touring BMW models. Like other BMW Boxers, it has a flat-twin engine and swing-arm suspension for both wheels, but there the similarities end. In the short-wheelbase frame sits a masterpiece of precision engineering with shaft and bevel drives to the twin overhead camshafts on both cylinder heads. This engine ruled the sidecar class in motorcycle racing for no less than twenty years, but today on the classic scene there seem to be more solo models around than ever before. And this could well be true with quite a few replicas having been assembled over the years.

A chance to ride a Rennsport BMW is a rare occasion for anybody other than a proud owner, but author Stefan Knittel is in a fortunate position to know one of these people quite well. One day the owner brought his precious racer to a secret test road in deep rural Bavaria. After he had warmed the engine up it was Knittel's turn. His reply when asked for a rev limit was simple: find out yourself!

Knittel expected run-and-bump starting to be difficult; it turned out to be the easiest thing to do—but then the engine stalled twice trying to get away. The secret is simple but hard to accept on a thirty-six-year-old racer worth a fortune. One has to rev up to 5000 rpm—the roar from the exhaust megaphone alone makes you shiver—and then slip the clutch and at the same time feed in more and more throttle action. Getting the knack of this takes some doing.

Knittel fixed his eyes onto the small tachometer so hard that he did not realize at first how much speed he had gained in the mean-time. As soon as the power is really on the revs go up alarmingly fast so that he had to change through the gears quickly every time the needle passed the 8000 rpm mark. It was a good idea to start at the beginning of a long straight, but in no time at all the sharp right turn was in sight and he grabbed the front brake lever only to find out that there was not the sort of response one would have expected on a Grand Prix racer. He had no choice but to shift down quickly and let the engine aid in slowing down the machine, which worked out quite well.

Now it was time to find a suitable riding position. The center of gravity is low down on a BMW flat twin, and lifting of the rear end must be kept in mind, as does the combination of light weight, short wheelbase and extremely narrow handlebars. As Knittel happens to be a tall Bavarian rider just like Schorsch Meier and Walter Zeller, he simply tried to copy their riding style which he had noted at numerous classic races over the years. This did the trick. Sitting well back, nearly on the seat hump, knees tucked into the recesses on the tank with a firm grip, crouching down over the tank, elbows in and only a light grasp on the handlebars, all steering is controlled from the shoulders. The position remains unaltered in all riding situations. One has in effect become a part of the machine.

Thereafter Knittel was able to enjoy what is the best flat-twin ever built—with the exception of Walter Zeller's own factory racer, which is a more developed version. It is not as easy to ride in comparison to a Manx Norton or a Guzzi racer from the same period, but it is a challenge second to none to ride it in a competitive way and it shows the talent of the rider in the saddle when fighting for the lead in a race.

Chapter 8

Sidecars and Accessories

You've finally found your BMW, you've checked it out, it looks good and runs good. Regardless of which model you've bought, you've now decided to send it back in time by either restoring it to showroom-stock original or by fitting it with some or all of the period accessories available at the time. Where do you begin? How will you know which of the hundreds of accessories are correct, which were most popular, and which will do the most to improve your BMW's looks and value?

BMW R75 with Steib sidecar and side boxes, here in Afrika Corps desert markings. Military accessories are especially difficult to find in the United States to finish an incomplete bike.

Sidecars

As often happens, the moment you discover that your pre 1970 BMW has built-in lugs for attaching a sidecar, you decide that you'll need one as well—especially after you've seen some of the beautiful rigs that show up at any gathering of BMW enthusiasts. The choice is practically limitless, and the availability in the United States of even the rarer, older models is still quite good and getting better all the time. Prices, on the other hand, have steadily increased as well, so that now a tin tub with only one wheel and no motor can often run you more than the BMW that will haul it.

For sheer fun alone, almost any sidecar, even a homebuilt, will do. For authenticity, the only proper hack is one of similar age as your BMW, preferably one made in Germany or Austria. Steib is still the sidecar of choice for many, with competing brands

from decades ago such as Bender, Felber, Nimbus, Stoye, Kali and others also quite popular and every bit as interesting.

The British Watsonian firm also built a quality sidecar, but since most came with a tiny wheel, fiberglass body and sometimes awkward styling, only a few Watsonians look all that good on older BMWs. An exception is the Jawa of Czechoslovakia, of which some of the earlier versions with 1950s styling look quite decent. The choice is yours.

Some modern-day reproductions of earlier designs are also good looking and not at all a detriment. These include the Ural from Russia, the Precision from France and the Globe from India, each of which looks like an uncanny copy of an earlier Steib or Stoye. Additionally, firms have now sprung up in Germany and in the United States which can reproduce virtually any sidecar ever built, right down to the last rivet and snap.

A rare combination indeed. This early postwar Steib TR500 is hooked up to an equally early 1952 R51/3. Only the mirrors are incorrect for the year, and the bar-end turn signals, with their elongated lens shape, are Japanese copies of the original German items made by Hella. *Vintage BMW Bulletin, Marie Lacko*

Remember, however, once you've found and learned to properly attach the sidecar of your dreams, your fun (and trouble) is just beginning. Unless you practice a totally new riding style, you'll quickly end up putting the sidecar into a parked car or signpost, which could spell an embarrassing and expensive end to your hobby. If all goes well, you'll next have to consider the purchase of sidecar gears for the BMW, possibly a hydraulic brake for the sidecar, wider handlebars, wheel rims and special sidecar-pattern tires, all of which will add at least another $1,000 to the sum you've already spent.

Your best bet is to join one of the many sidecar clubs, where help can be found and contacts made. At the very least join one of the major BMW clubs where you'll find several sidecars for sale each month in the classifieds section of their magazines. There is a list of sources for parts and complete sidecars in both the United States as well as Europe at the back of this book.

Accessories

As for the normal period accessories that do so much to make the bike look right, the picture is much more complex, and finding even a few items, such as solo saddles, lights and mirrors, can be both frustrating and expensive. Happily, the availability of virtually anything once fitted to any BMW built prior to 1970 is now quite good, which was not always the case even a few short years

More precious metal, in the shape of a BMW R60/2 and Spezial sidecar. The BMW is fitted with an aluminum-alloy Heinrich fairing and Albert mirrors, while the sidecar carries a seldom-seen Richter Kabine canopy and windshield. *Vintage BMW Bulletin, Jonathan Hayt*

Although S Series bullet-nosed Steib sidecars are the ones most commonly seen attached to pre 1970 BMWs, this look-alike is a Bender, built to similar quality standards in Denmark from the 1930s through the 1960s. While the large single road light on the sidecar chassis is a modern addition, the Hella signals, Albert headlamp mirrors, headlight guard, VDO tachometer and Craven pannier cases are all proper period accessories. *Vintage BMW Bulletin, Marie Lacko*

What better way to come a-calling during the holidays than with this 1969 R69S and late 1970s Russian built Ural sidecar, which was a close copy of the Steib military item built during World War II. *Vintage BMW Bulletin, Allan S. Atherton*

All-white combinations are still a rarity, especially ones as nicely outfitted as this R60/2 and Steib S-501. The pinstriping scheme on the sidecar gives you an idea why these models are often referred to as the Cucumber Steibs. The period accessories include two Hella bar-end signals and a pair of Hella spotlamp mirrors, large 6½ gallon gas tank, solo and pillion saddles, and headlight guard. *Vintage BMW Bulletin, Rich Sheckler*

Quite correct in nearly all respects is this 1952 R51/3 and Steib LS200 combination. The characteristic "cobra" handle on the sidecar fender shows this is a Steib and not a BMW Standard. The BMW is fitted with a single Albert bar-end mirror, the correct 1952 fishtails, iron drums with shrunk-on ribs, small taillamp and stamped-steel parcel rack. Only the rabid purist would note the use of a 1950 R51/2 gas tank, which had a sideways-opening toolbox, instead of the proper 1952 item, where the lock is at the middle top of the lid. *Vintage BMW Bulletin, Jonathan Hayt*

A nice original early Ural, recognized by its small fender lamp, mounted to an R60/2. The lamp has been upgraded with chrome, and the sidecar's seat has been treated to a modern cover, both improvements over the utilitarian Russian military items. *Vintage BMW Bulletin, Marie Lacko*

ago. Many club members and private firms are now manufacturing new, or importing the occasionally found new-old-stock parts and accessories. All advertise regularly in the BMW club magazines.

If you have to add something, start with mirrors, of which there are at least four different styles, from handlebar- to headlight-mount, to bar-end and even spotlamp-mirror combinations. Avoid the larger modern items, which may be good from a standpoint of safety, but look wrong on a forty-year-old BMW. Common names on the classic mirrors are Albert, Hagus or Talbot, all from Germany.

Next you might want a fairing, such as the excellent British Avon, or the rarer and more-expensive two-piece Heinrich and its many variations. All these fairings shroud the engine and tank, which can lead to reflected engine noise, as well as some danger of overheating at low road speeds, so think

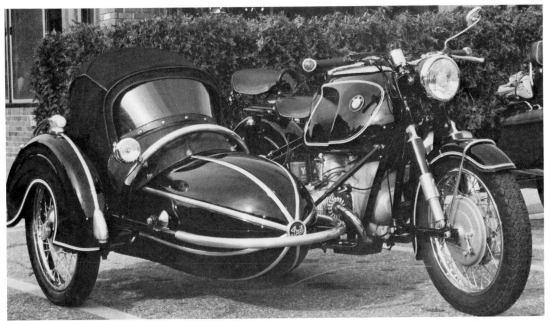

R60/2 with Steib S-500, complete with claustrophobic canvas top and Hella spotlamp mirrors. Nice touches are the Heinrich gas tank, VDO tachometer in chrome versus the usual black, Hella bar-end signals, extra-capacity oil-pan and clamp-on aluminum exhaust port fins. *Vintage BMW Bulletin, Marie Lacko*

before you buy. Modern fairings, such as the Pichler or the new Peel vintage lookalike also work quite well, as they are based on designs popular twenty or more years ago.

After the fairings, there are gas tanks large and small, with some downright monstrous in capacity. The 10 or even 12 gallon tanks look good only on a BMW it seems. Tanks by Hoske are generally slab-sided and mirror the shape of earlier Rennsport tanks, of which Hoske was a supplier; Heinrich tanks look humpbacked and whale-like in comparison. Each have their devotees, and both new and used examples are readily available. There's also the optional 6½ gallon Sport tank from BMW or Schorsch Meier, which fits most BMWs prior to 1970.

You may also want to think about saddlebags or panniers. For many, only the period tall, square, leather Denfeld bags will do, while others prefer British Craven items, which are again being produced in a bewil-

Looking all the world like a casket belonging to an undertaker who prefers his BMW over his hearse, this is in fact a seldom-seen Steib LT200 Delivery Box. Showpiece in Bob Henig's BMW spares shop, this little sidecar measured 57x15x15 in. and could carry a load of 243 lb. Three decades ago, these were a common sight in every major European city, where they hauled everything from beer to newspapers. Finding one in the United States today is well nigh impossible. *Bob Henig*

Vintage R69US tourer in the correct dress for 1969, with US telescopics, Avon Avonaire fairing, Albert handlebar mirrors, Craven Golden Arrow luggage cases and small top box. *Vintage BMW Bulletin, Richard Kahn*

Two views of some desirable Heinrich products, both fitted to R69S BMWs. The one on the left has the two-piece lightweight aluminum-alloy fairing, with the lower portion designed to drop over the standard 4 gallon tank. The BMW on the right has a large Heinrich gas tank and just the handlebar fairing. Albert mirrors and Hella signals complete the picture. *Karl Heinrich*

To complete your restoration of a pre 1930s BMW, you may want one of these Bosch reproductions from Germany. The one here looks better than new, and will cost several hundred dollars. *Vintage BMW Bulletin, Randy Franks*

Typical display of the mid 1960s, as set up by the US importer at that time, Butler and Smith. The mannequin wearing the funny smile and the Belstaff rainsuit seems to be enjoying himself behind a nice two-piece Heinrich fairing. In spite of their aluminum construction, these could take a lot of abuse, and it's still possible to find ones from 30 years ago at flea markets that are in relatively good condition. *Vintage BMW Bulletin, Richard Kahn*

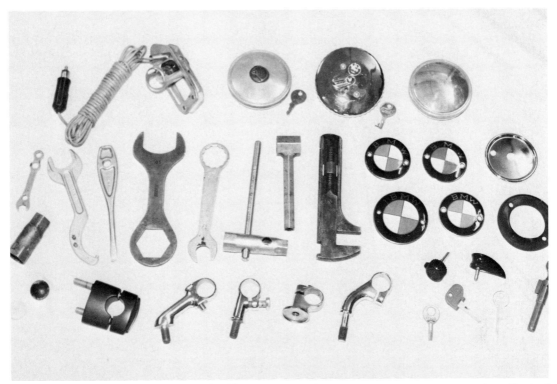

More readily available, in both the United States and Germany, are these items. Starting at the bottom, there are various toolbox, fork and ignition keys, plus handlebar risers for five different series spanning more than 35 years. Among the tools are some rare prewar wrenches, flanked by pre- and postwar tank emblems, gas caps—even a trouble light, which fits into the little socket under the seat of pre 1970 BMWs. *Bob Henig*

dering variety, or the teardrop Enduro bags favored by many American riders in the 1960s.

It's virtually impossible to tell the new from the original accessories, so good are some of the reproductions. While some may be quite expensive, others are still pegged at bargain prices. In all cases, most will save you time, money and aggravation that you'd otherwise be spending trying to restore some badly abused item. Again, a few of the major sources are listed at the back of this book.

Remember, don't add too much. Your BMW, after all, came into this world naked, and to many it still looks the best with only a mirror as an accessory. Add only what appeals to you, not what you think you need, or what the other riders next to you have added to theirs. Like many things in this world, too much of a good thing can be bad for you, and your BMW.

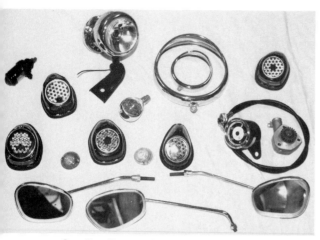

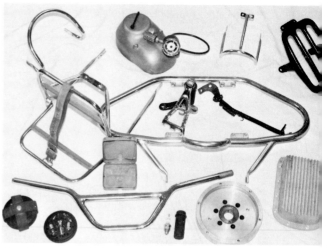

Small taillamps for pre 1955 BMWs, as well as for sidecars. Albert mirrors, Hella signals and spotlamp-mirrors, plus an oil-pump-driven VDO tachometer setup are also available. *Bob Henig*

Another version of the VDO tachometer assembly, this time for the 1951–56 models with camshaft-driven tachometer gearbox, plus headlight, taillight and cylinder guards, an Akip sidestand, plus one for an R27, a special flywheel and a deep oil pan, even some prewar bulb kits for that final touch. *Bob Henig*

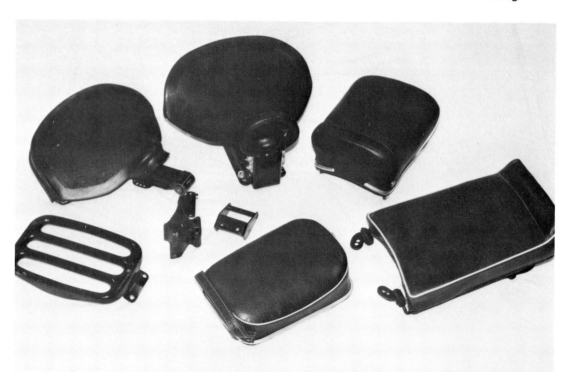

Four styles of pillion pads and saddles, a rack to mount them on, plus a swinging pillion pad and the solo saddle it attaches to. It's these small details that can turn an otherwise excellent BMW into a real head turner. *Bob Henig*

144

Much of the touring equipment from this R100RT can be ordered through BMW dealers and mounted on other models. Many accessories are interchangeable between later models, and other equipment is available from numerous aftermarket and BMW dealerships, such as Luftmeister in the United States.

Chapter 9

The BMW Scene

Among today's motorcycle manufacturers not too many can look back on a long illustrious history that reaches to the early decades of the century. Harley-Davidson's unbroken run of production goes back as far as 1903, Moto Guzzi started in 1921 and BMW in 1923, long before the giants from the Orient. Other than with certain British models, it took longer for BMW motorcycles from past periods to be considered as collector's items. This may partly be due to the fact that they were all too rare outside of the Fatherland. In Germany black BMW singles and flat twins were such a common sight well into the 1970s that the difference between a prewar and a more recent model was not generally known, noticed or of any great interest. There have always been specialists in the past who have taken a greater interest than others, but a true enthusiast following that would lead to the formation of collectors and enthusiast clubs was not established until the end of the 1970s in Germany; many feel it had its origins in the United States in 1972.

There are two large BMW clubs that are devoted to the collector's side of BMW motorcycles, in counterpoint to a worldwide net of BMW rider's clubs in general. The older of the two is the Vintage BMW Owners Club in the United States, which was founded in 1972. It is easy to understand why the German BMW Veteranen Club has developed a much bigger following, for it is comprised of sections for cars and motorcycles, and is to some extent directly supported by the factory. Quite an extensive list of remanufactured parts for BMW motorcycles from the 1920s and 1930s is part of the club's services in addition to rallies and club activities. Owners of later models, too, are well represented in both the American and German clubs, of course.

In Germany, with so many BMW models from the 1950s and 1960s still around, and with so many owners still wanting to restore and use them, the BMW factory is more than willing to provide assistance. A small scale supply business and occasional remanufacturing has always been handled through legendary works rider Schorsch Meier's shop in Munich. His worldwide reputation on one hand, and good contacts with the necessary departments at the factory on the other, helped to make this possible.

With the start of the vintage motorcycle movement, this casual way of dealing would soon need to be put on a much firmer basis. Instead of handing the organization over to the clubs, the BMW Motorcycle Division realized that such an increased demand would be too much for a club to handle, no matter how well organized, and decided to concentrate the remanufacturing of parts at a small business in northern Germany, where this sort of production had been done previously on a private basis. Paffen KG at Varel supplies the parts to the official BMW

Typical of the many gatherings of BMW enthusiasts in the United States, this BMWMOA rally at Table Rock, South Carolina, attracted over 800 BMW motorcycles back in 1974. Today, such annual affairs generally can expect to have 5,000 attendees. *Vintage BMW Bulletin, Richard Kahn*

Spare Parts Division, from where every factory appointed dealer in the world can order parts for out-of-production machines. This setup has not yet been well publicized, as not everybody at the BMW dealer level is too happy about it, since they prefer to sell new models and accessories, but the responsible people in Munich invite BMW motorcycle owners to use the system as much as possible, and report their requirements and their criticism.

All this does not mean that there are no other sources for BMW parts. Independent specialists in Germany, the United States, England and other countries as well operate quite successfully with their own programs. Many usable secondhand spares are available through swap meet dealers.

On the American side of the ocean, both the longtime BMW enthusiast and the novice collector no longer need to look to Germany as their only source of parts and information. Predating the German Veteranen Club by a few years, the major US club catering solely to owners and restorers of pre 1970 BMWs is the Vintage BMW Motorcycle Owners, Ltd., which was founded by two enthusiasts in February of 1972. From its humble beginnings with just seventeen members, the club enters the 1990s with over 4,000 members, of which over half still take an active part in the club's success. The club's newsletter, *Vintage BMW Bulletin*, is devoted to technical features, illustrated historical articles and classified ads, where every model of every BMW ever built, from the R32 to the Reg Pridmore racer, has at one time or other been offered for sale.

While the Vintage Club is not as structured as its German counterpart, with a working staff of only two or three volunteer members, and with no organized spare parts remanufacturing scheme such as is available in Germany, it has nevertheless given impetus to numerous successful spares businesses, all of which exist to serve the needs of BMW enthusiasts worldwide. The successful and far-reaching enterprises of several club members, which can now provide everything from a taillight lens to a complete machine, have done much to keep many a neglected BMW from ending up as a parts bike and to be cannibalized of every remaining piece until nothing of value remains. The Vintage Club holds a number of small-scale rallies, get-togethers and swap meets in the eastern United States, Missouri, Wisconsin and California. At these events members can exchange ideas, buy and sell parts, and ride and admire their machines. Few of the members are simply collectors or investors, however. The Vintage Club still holds to its

The second Vintage BMW Owners get-together, at a private airfield in Mason, New Hampshire, also in 1974. Some of these BMWs, even then already over 20 years old, came from as far away as Ohio, and most of the people pictured are still active members today. *Vintage BMW Bulletin, Richard Pogue*

The usual setting of the small US Vintage Club meets will probably involve a wooded campsite and a lake, as seen here at a recent meet in Massachusetts. In the foreground, an R60/2 with Steib S–501, while in the background, an R67/2, still with its original Munich plate, attached to a BMW Spezial sidecar. *Vintage BMW Bulletin, Marie Lacko*

original credo, that the "preservation, enjoyment and use of vintage and classic BMW motorcycles" is its main purpose.

The Vintage Club also enjoys a good relationship with BMW of North America, the US importer of cars and motorcycles, as well as with Munich, and owes much of its success to assistance it received in its early years from members such as Hans Fleischmann, former head of the BMW archives, and to journalists like Dr. Helmut Krackowizer of the Zweirad-Archiv in Austria.

In addition to the Vintage Club, there are two other large BMW motorcycle clubs worth joining, known as the BMW Motorcycle Owners of America (BMWMOA) and the BMW Riders Association (BMWRA). The former caters primarily to the BMW touring and camping enthusiast, while the latter to the rider-enthusiast as well as those more concerned with technical issues and news of new model developments coming out of Germany. Both publish excellent newsletters and both hold at least one large rally each year, which can draw thousands of participants from all over the world. Unlike the Vintage Club, BMWRA and BMWMOA each have numerous local and regional chapters, any of which may in turn also publish a newsletter and hold their own rallies and events. All three clubs enjoy the support of BMW of North America and each has developed its own contacts with the factory in Munich.

There is also another club, the BMW Vintage Club of America, which has even closer ties to the German Veteranen Club, but it deals solely with antique and classic BMW cars from the 1920s through the late 1960s. Both it and Vintage BMW Motorcycle Owners, Ltd., share information whenever possible and promote each other's efforts. Many BMW enthusiasts are members of both.

Finally, a number of Vintage Club members, both in the United States and Canada, as well as in Germany and England, own and regularly campaign restored BMW racers at vintage racing events. Collectively they may race original factory Kompressor Rennsports, postwar sidecar outfits or an occasional RS54 solo machine, all of which helps keep BMW's past racing successes fresh in mind, making them as much a part of today's vintage scene as any gathering of vintage BMW enthusiasts. It is to all of these people, the racers, restorers, collectors and riders, who all enjoy to the fullest the enduring quality that BMW motorcycles have stood for since 1923, and who happily share this enthusiasm with newcomers to the hobby, that the BMW vintage scene in the United States and across the seas owes its greatest success.

Specifications and Production

Specifications of BMW motorcycles 1923–90

Years	Model	Cylinders	Bore x stroke	CC	Hp/rpm	Production
1923–26	R32	2	68 x 68 mm	494	8,5/3300	3,090
1925–26	R37	2	68 x 68	494	16/4000	152
1925–26	R39	1	68 x 68	247	6,5/4000	855
1926–28	R42	2	68 x 68	494	12/3400	6,502
1927–28	R47	2	68 x 68	494	18/4000	1,720
1928–29	R52	2	68 x 68	494	12/3400	4,377
1928–30	R57	2	68 x 68	494	18/4000	1,006
1928–29	R62	2	78 x 78	745	18/3400	4,355
1928–29	R63	2	83 x 68	735	24/4000	794
1929–33 1934	R11	2	78 x 78	745	18/3400 20/4000	7,500
1929–31 1932–34	R16	2	83 x 68	735	25/4000 33/4000	1,106
1931–33 1934–36	R2	1	63 x 64	198	6/3500 8/4500	15,207
1932–33 1934–37	R4	1	78 x 84	398	12/3500 14/4200	15,295
1936	R3	1	68 x 84	305	11/4200	740
1935–42	R12	2	78 x 78	745	18/3400 20/4000	36,008
1935–37	R17	2	83 x 68	735	33/5000	434
1936–37	R5	2	68 x 68	494	24/5800	2,652
1937	R6	2	70 x 78	596	18/4800	1,850
1937–40	R35	1	72 x 84	342	14/4500	15,386
1937–38	R20	1	60 x 68	192	8/5400	5,000
1938–40	R23	1	68 x 68	247	10/5400	9,021
1938–40	R51	2	68 x 68	494	24/5600	3,775
1938–41	R66	2	70 x 78	597	30/5300	1,669
1938–41	R61	2	70 x 78	597	18/4800	3,747
1938–41	R71	2	78 x 78	745	22/4600	3,458
1941–44	R75	2	78 x 78	745	26/4000	ca. 18,000
1948–50	R24	1	68 x 68	247	12/5600	12,020
1950–51	R25	1	68 x 68	247	12/5600	23,400
1951–53	R25/2	1	68 x 68	247	12/5600	38,651
1953–56	R25/3	1	68 x 68	247	13/5800	47,700
1950–51	R51/2	2	68 x 68	494	24/5800	5,000
1951–54	R51/3	2	68 x 68	494	24/5800	18,420
1951	R67	2	72 x 73	594	26/5500	1,470

Years	Model	Cylinders	Bore x stroke	CC	Hp/rpm	Production
1952–54	R67/2	2	72 x 73	594	28/5600	4,234
1955–56	R67/3	2	72 x 73	594	28/5600	700
1952–54	R68	2	72 x 73	594	35/7000	1,452
1955–60	R50	2	68 x 68	494	26/5800	13,510
1960–69	R50/2	2	68 x 68	494	26/5800	19,036
1955–60	R69	2	72 x 73	594	35/6800	2,956
1956–60	R60	2	72 x 73	594	28/5600	3,530
1960–69	R60/2	2	72 x 73	594	30/5800	17,306
1956–60	R26	1	68 x 68	247	15/6400	30,236
1960–66	R27	1	68 x 68	247	18/7400	15,364
1960–62	R50S	2	68 x 68	494	35/7650	1,634
1960–69	R69S	2	72 x 73	594	42/7000	11,317
1969–73	R50/5	2	67 x 70.6	496	32/6400	7,865
1969–73	R60/5	2	73.5 x 70.6	599	40/6400	22,721
1969–73	R75/5	2	82 x 70.6	745	50/6200	38,370
1973–76	R90/6	2	90 x 70.6	898	60/6500	21,070
1973–76	R90S	2	90 x 70.6	898	67/7000	17,455
1973–76	R60/6	2	73.5 x 70.6	599	40/6400	13,511
1973–76	R75/6	2	82 x 70.6	745	50/6200	17,587
1976–80	R60/7	2	73.5 x 70.6	599	40/6400	11,163
1976–77	R75/7	2	82 x 70.6	745	50/6200	6,264
	R80/7	2	84.8 x 70.6	797	50/7250	
1977–84					55/7000	18,552
1976–78	R100/7	2	94 x 70.6	980	60/6500	12,056
1976–78	R100S	2	94 x 70.6	980	65/6600	9,657
1976–84	R100RS	2	94 x 70.6	980	70/7250	33,648
1978–84	R100RT	2	94 x 70.6	980	70/7250	13,516
1978–84	R100T	2	94 x 70.6	980	65/7250	21,928
1980–84	R100CS	2	94 x 70.6	980	70/7000	6,141
1978–85	R45	2	70 x 61.5	473	27/6500	28,158
1978–80	R65	2	82 x 61.5	649	45/7250	
1980–85					50/7250	29,454
1981–85	R65LS	2	82 x 61.5	649	50/7250	6,389
1980–87	R80G/S	2	84.8 x 70.6	797	50/6500	21,864
1982–84	R80ST	2	84.8 x 70.6	797	50/6500	5,963
1982–84	R80RT	2	84.8 x 70.6	797	50/6500	7,315
1983–89	K100	4	67 x 70	987	90/8000	12,717
1983–89	K100RS	4	67 x 70	987	90/8000	35,562
1984–88	K100RT	4	67 x 70	987	90/8000	22,332
1986–	K100LT	4	67 x 70	987	90/8000	9,790 (12/89)
1986–	K75	3	67 x 70	740	75/8500	6,703 (12/89)
1985–88	K75C	3	67 x 70	740	75/8500	9,266
1986–	K75S	3	67 x 70	740	75/8500	11,576 (12/89)
1985–	R65	2	82 x 61.5	649	48/7250	6,869 (12/89)
1984–	R80	2	84 x 70.6	798	50/6500	10,147 (12/89)
1984–	R80RT	2	84 x 70.6	798	50/6500	15,213 (12/89)
1986–89	R100RS	2	94 x 70.6	980	60/6500	4,397
1987–	R100RT	2	94 x 70.6	980	60/6500	3,239 (12/89)
1988–	R65GS	2	82 x 61.5	649	27/5500	619 (12/89)
1987–	R80GS	2	84 x 70.6	798	50/6500	3,235 (12/89)
1988–	R100GS	2	94 x 70.6	980	60/6500	10,356 (12/89)
1989–	K1	4	67 x 70	987	100/8000	NA
1990–	K100RS	4	67 x 70	987	100/8000	3,586 (12/89)
1990–	K75RT	3	67 x 70	740	75/8500	NA

Engine numbers of BMW motorcycles 1923–73

Years	Model	Engine numbers	Remarks
1923–26	R32	31000–34100	First BMW motorcycle
1925–26	R37	35001–35175	First ohv engine
1925–26	R39	36000–36900	First BMW single
1926–28	R42	40001–46999	
1927–28	R47	34201–35999	
1928–29	R52	47000–51383	
1928–30	R57	70001–71012	
1928–29	R62	60001–65000	First 750 sv engine
1928–29	R63	75001–76000	First 750 ohv engine
1929–30	R11 Series I	60001–65000	First Star frame
1930–31	R11 Series II	65001–66900	
1931–32	R11 Series III	67500–68751	
1932–33	R11 Series III+	68752–68920	
1933	R11 Series IV	69001–70122	
1934	R11 Series V	70123–73984	
1929–30	R16 Series I	75001–76000	
1930–32	R16 Series II	76001–76700	
1932	R16 Series III		First twin carburetors
1933	R16 Series IV	76701–76851	
1934	R16 Series V	76852–76953	
1931	R2 Series I	101–4260	First Star single
1932	R2 Series II	4261–6276	
1933	R2 Series II '33	6277–8113	
1934	R2 Series III	8114–10201	
1935	R2 Series IV	10202–12901	
1936	R2 Series V	12902–14816	
1936	R3	106001–106740	
1932	R4 Series I	80001–81110	Largest BMW single
1933	R4 Series II	81111–82838	
1934	R4 Series III	82839–86563	
1935	R4 Series IV	86601–90250	
1936–37	R4 Series V	90251–95280	
1937–40	R35	300001–315387	
1935–37	R12	501–24199	First telescopic forks
	R12 Twin-carb	(Within above)	
1937–42	R12 Military	25001–37161	
1935–37	R17	77001–77436	
1937–38	R20	100001–105004	Tubular frames
1938–40	R23	106001–114021	
1936–37	R5	(1936)8001–9503; (1937)500001–502786	
1937	R6	600001–601850	
1938–40	R51	503001–506172	Plunger rear suspension
1938–41	R61	603001–606080; (1941)607001–607340	
1938–40	R66	660001–661629	
1941	R66	662001–662039	
1938–39	R71	700005–702200	
1941	R71	703001–703511	
1941–44	R75	750001–above 768000	Driven sidecar

Years	Model	Engine numbers	Remarks
1948–50	R24	200009–212007	First postwar BMW
1950–51	R25	220001–243400	Plungers added
1951–54	R25/2	245001–283650	
1953–56	R25/3	284001–331705	
1950–51	R51/2	516001–521005	First postwar twin
1951–54	R51/3	522001–540950	
1951	R67	610001–611449	First postwar 600 cc
1952–54	R67/2	6120001–616226	
1955–56	R67/3	617001–617700	
1952–54	R68	650001–651453	First sport BMW
1956–60	R26	340001–370236	First swing-arm single
1960–66	R27	372001–387566	Rubber-mounted engine
1955–60	R50	550001–563515	First swing-arm twin
1960–69	R50/2	630001–649037	
1967–69	R50US	(Within above)	US telescopics
1960–62	R50S	564005–565639	Hot 500 cc
1956–60	R60	618001–621530	First swing-arm 600
1960–69	R60/2	622001–629999	
1967–69	R60US	(Within above)	US telescopics
1955–60	R69	652001–654955	Hot 600 cc
1960–69	R69S	655004–666320	Raised compression
1968–69	R69US	(Within above)	US telescopics
1969–73	R50/5	2900001–2903623	Revamped 1970s Line
1969–73	R60/5	2930001–2938704	
1969–73	R75/5	2970001–2982737	First 750 cc since 1941

Total production of BMW motorcycles 1923–89

Year	Production	Year	Production
1923	Handful of R32 prototypes	1940	16,211
1924	ca. 1,500	1941	ca. 10,250
1925	1,640	1942	ca 7,000
1926	2,360	1943	ca. 7,000
1927	3,397	1944	ca. 2,000
1928	4,932	1945	0
1929	5,680	1946	0
		1947	0
1930	ca. 6,000	1948	59
1931	6,681	1949	9,400
1932	4,652		
1933	4,734	1950	17,061
1934	9,689	1951	25,101
1935	10,005	1952	28,310
1936	11,922	1953	27,704
1937	12,549	1954	29,699
1938	17,300	1955	23,531
1939	21,667	1956	15,500

Year	Production	Year	Production
1957	5,429	1973	15,078
1958	7,156	1974	23,160
1959	8,412	1975	25,566
		1976	28,209
1960	9,473	1977	31,515
1961	9,460	1978	29,580
1962	4,302	1979	24,415
1963	6,043		
1964	9,043	1980	29,260
1965	7,118	1981	33,120
1966	9,071	1982	30,559
1967	7,896	1983	28,048
1968	5,074	1984	34,001
1969	4,701	1985	37,104
		1986	32,054
1970	12,287	1987	27,508
1971	18,772	1988	23,817
1972	21,122	1989	25,750

Sources

Parts sources

The following is a brief list of sources in the United States for new, used or reproduction BMW parts and accessories, as well as sidecars and restoration services. This list is current as of spring 1990. The authors realize that this list is far from complete, and apologize for any omissions. The latest sources for parts and suppliers will always be listed in the publications of the US BMW clubs. We have omitted the dozens of major German and European suppliers, but these can be found in the advertising sections of the German and British magazines.

Accessory Mart, Inc.
P.O. Box 26116
Cincinnatti, OH 45226
Excellent source of new, used, obsolete British and German parts, complete machines and sidecars. A comprehensive illustrated catalog is published periodically.

American Jawa, Ltd.
185 Express St.
Plainview, NY 11803
Importer of Jawa, Velorex sidecars and accessories.

Bing Agency International
824 South Broad
Fremont, NE 68025
US distributor of German Bing carburetors and repair parts.

Bley Vintage Engineering
700 Chase
Elk Grove, IL 60007
Emphasis on vintage racing, as well as quality machine-shop work and complete restorations.

Blue Moon Cycle
5711 Woodvalley Trace
Norcross, GA 30071
Seller of new and used BMW parts.

BMW Motorrad St. Louis/Sidecar Restorations
4011 Forest Park Blvd.
St. Louis, MO 63108
Importer of EML sidecars. Also sells vintage sidecars, parts, accessories and BMW motorcycles.

Bob's Used Parts
10630 Riggs Hill Rd., Unit Y
Jessup, MD 20794
Importer of new, used, obsolete and reproduction BMW parts and accessories, sidecars and the occasional prewar BMW motorcycle. The most complete selection anywhere.

Buchanan Frame
629 East Garvey
Monterey Park, CA 91754
Quality spoke and wheel service, with reproduction spokes in stainless steel the specialty.

California BMW
2490 Old Middlefield Way
Mt. View, CA 94043
  BMW dealer, provider of excellent parts and service for most postwar BMWs.

Capital Cycle Corporation
1508 Moran Dr.
Sterling, VA 22170
  Catalog sales and service, for most post 1955 BMWs and the parts required to keep them running.

C & D BMW, Inc.
1280 IL 75 East
Freeport, IL 61032
  BMW dealer and provider of excellent parts, service and machine-shop work.

Competition Accessories, Inc.
P.O. Box 160
Xenia, OH 45385
  Seller of parts and accessories for post 1970 BMWs as provided direct from BMW of North America.

David Quinn Motorcycles
335 Litchfield Turnpike
Bethany, CT 06525
  Importer and distributor for Craven bags, Belstaff clothing and Avon fairings.

Ed Korn
170 Jackson St.
Madison, WI 53704
  Fabricates virtually all special repair tools for postwar BMWs, and has produced two excellent repair videos dealing with pre 1970 BMWs.

EPCO, Inc.
RR 4, Box 179
Germantown, OH 45327
  Manufacturer of stainless steel BMW exhaust pipes.

Frank's Maintenance and Engineering
945 Pitner Ave.
Evanston, IL 60602
  Manufacturer of fork tubes.

Hannigan Fairings and Sidecars
121 Speers Rd.
Oakville, Ontario L6L 2X4
Canada
  Distributor of Hannigan fairings, sidecars and accessories.

Irv's Speedometer Hospital
3810 Collier Rd.
Randallstown, MD 21133
  Repairs speedometers and tachometers.

Jim Young
Box 537
North Pembroke, MA 02358
  Importer of custom-made replica exhaust pipes and mufflers in stainless steel for virtually any old or new BMW or other classic.

Kieth's Touring Specialties
483 Liberty Ave.
Jersey City, NJ 07307
  Sells proven and tested touring, camping and other BMW accessories.

Luftmeister, Inc.
15932 A Downey Ave.
Paramount, CA 90723
  Distributor of fairings and accessories for most modern BMWs.

Motorrad Elektrik
Rt. 12, Box 53
Gadsden, AL 35901
  Repairs, rebuilds and offers 6 volt to 12 volt conversions for older BMWs.

Palo Alto Speedometer
718 Emerson
Palo Alto, CA 94301
  Quality speedometer and tachometer repairs, and instrument face restorations.

Peel TT Touring
Ian M. MacKintosh
33931 Diana Dr.
Dana Point, CA 92629
  Manufacturer and distributor of a quality vintage Peel fairing replica, for pre 1970 BMW motorcycles.

Pichler
196 S. VanBuren Ave.
Barberton, OH 44023
   Importer and distributor of German Pichler fairings.

Randy Franks
10524 White Oak Ave.
Granada Hills, CA 91344
   Distributor of original and reprint BMW literature and prewar BMW parts.

Watsonian Sidecars
c/o Doug Bingham/Sidestrider, Inc.
15838 Arminta St., Unit 25
Van Nuys, CA 91406
   Importer and distributor of British Watsonian sidecars and accessories.

American BMW clubs

   The following are some of the more prominent clubs and organizations in the United States devoted wholly or in part to the use and enjoyment of BMW motorcycles. While some also concern themselves with all brands of motorcycles, or just limit themselves to what we now consider antiques, all can be an excellent source of assistance, information, camaraderie and an excellent way to find, through the classifieds in their various publications, that BMW you've always wanted.

Antique Motorcycle Club of America, Inc.
P.O. Box 333
Sweetser, IN 46987
   Founded 1954, and devoted to all brands of antique and classic motorcycles. They publish an excellent quality color magazine, *The Antique Motorcycle*. The AMC has numerous national chapters and events.

BMW Motorcycle Owners of America, Inc.
P.O. Box 489
Chesterfield, MO 63006-0489
   Founded 1971, and concerned primarily with touring and rallies. Their magazine, *BMW Owners News*, has an extensive classified section. BMWMOA has many national chapters and events.

BMW Riders Association
P.O. Box 1613
Lufkin, TX 75902-1613
   Founded 1971, and devoted primarily to the riding and enjoyment of BMW motorcycles, with considerable emphasis on technical and future BMW development. The BMWRA publication is *On the Level*. BMWRA has numerous regional chapters and national events.

BMW Vintage Club of America, Inc.
16290 Kelly Cove Dr. #258
Ft. Myers, FL 33908
   Founded 1975. While concerned primarily with the various out-of-production automobiles built by BMW in both Munich and Eisenach, the club shares information with Vintage BMW Motorcycle Owners, Ltd. and many members are affiliated with both clubs. The club newsletter, *The BMW Vintage Bulletin*, covers cars built prior to the 1970s.

Deutsches Motorrad Register
8663 Grover Place
Shreveport, LA 71115
   Founded in 1982, and concerned with the dissemination of information on all motorcycles built in Germany. An excellent source of contact for members with unusual or limited-production machines. The club is US distributor for *Markt fur Klassische Automobile und Motorrader*, an excellent German-language magazine dealing with vintage vehicles with an illustrated classifieds section.

United Sidecar Association, Inc.
P.O. Box 1353
Homewood, IL 60430-0353
   Founded 1979, and concerned with sidecars and their history. Classified ads in the US publication, *The Sidecarist*.

Vintage BMW Motorcycle Owners, Ltd.
P.O. Box 67
Exeter, NH 03833
   Founded 1972, and devoted to the preservation, enjoyment and use of antique (1923-1945), vintage (1948-1954), classic (1955-1969), and contemporary (post 1970) BMW motorcycles. Members worldwide, with several annual rallies and events in the

United States. The VBMWMO publication, *Vintage BMW Bulletin*, is a bimonthly, illustrated magazine covering historical, technical and rally features, with a classified section for BMWs.

BMW factory and European BMW clubs
BMW of North America, Inc.
Public Relations
P.O. Box 1227
Westwood, NJ 07675

Bayerische Motoren Werke AG
Postfach 40 02 40
D–8000 Munchen 40
Germany

BMW Motorrad GmbH
Triebstr. 32
D–8000 Munchen 50
Germany

BMW Clubs Europa e.V.
Herrn Wolfgang Marx
Petuelring 130
D–8000 Munchen 40
Germany

BMW Veteranen Club Deutschland
Im Breiten Feld 19
D–5910 Kreuztal-Kredenbach
West Germany

Intern. Verband der BMW Clubs
Lierberg 7–A
D–4330 Muelheim/R
West Germany

The BMW Club
Peter Kyle
1 Barrowsfield
South Croydon, Surrey CR2 9EA
England

The Vintage Motor Cycle Club, Ltd.
138 Derby Street
Burton-on-Trent,
Staffs. DE14 2LF
England

BMW and related motorcycle publications
Some of the major and most popular publications which deal specifically with BMW motorcycles, as well as those which, on a regular basis, devote time and space to the restoration and repair of BMWs and other classics are listed here.

The Antique Motorcycle, published quarterly by the Antique Motorcycle Club of America, Inc., Richard J. Schunk, editor. Beautiful color magazine, with excellent classified ads. To join the AMC, write Dick Winger, P.O. Box 333, Sweetser, IN 46987.

BMW Owners News, published monthly by BMW Motorcycle Owners of America, Inc. Devoted to the BMW rally and touring enthusiast, with classified ads for BMWs, sidecars and other makes. To join BMWMOA, contact BMW Motorcycle Owners of America, Inc., P.O. Box 489, Chesterfield, MO 63006–0489.

Classic Bike, *The Classic Motorcycle*, *Classic Mechanics* and *Classic Racer*, all British magazines of excellent quality and content, with detailed advertisements. Distributed in the United States by *Motorsport*, 550 Honey Locust Rd., Jonesburg, MO 63351–9600.

Hack'D, a periodical concerned with sidecars and the hobby, Jim Dodson, editor. Available from P.O. Box T, Woodbridge, VA 22194.

Hemmings Motor News, published monthly, at Box 100, Bennington, VT 05201. Large, comprehensive classified advertising magazine dealing primarily with automobiles, but which now has a motorcycle section.

The Bike Journal, published monthly, at P.O. Box 391, Mt. Morris, IL 61054–7906. New magazine with classified ads arranged by country of manufacture, and also featuring technical and racing articles, and extensive photographs.

On the Level, published monthly by BMW Riders Association, Robert Hellman, editor. Main emphasis is the riding, enjoyment and use of BMW motorcycles, with considerable coverage of technical features and future BMW developments, provided by sources close to the factory. To join BMWRA, contact BMW Riders Association, P.O. Box 1613, Lufkin, TX 75902–1613.

Rider. Slick newsstand publication, which covers all brands as well as BMW. To subscribe, contact P.O. Box 51901, Boulder, CO 80321–1901.

Road Rider. The original touring and camping magazine, with considerable BMW emphasis and excellent, free classifieds. Contact P.O. Box 488, Mt. Morris, IL 61054–0488.

Sidecarist, published by the United Sidecar Association. The magazine is concerned with the use and fitment of sidecars to all brands of motorcycles, and has comprehensive classified ads. To join, contact United Sidecar Association, Inc., P.O. Box 1353, Homewood, IL 60430–0353.

Vintage BMW Bulletin, published bi monthly by Vintage BMW Motorcycle Owners, Ltd., Roland Slabon, editor. An illustrated magazine devoted to the preservation, enjoyment and use of pre 1970 BMW motorcycles. Classified advertising free to members, which covers all years of BMW production, sidecars and other classic makes. To join VBMWMO, Ltd., write to P.O. Box 67, Exeter, NH 03833.

Walneck's Classic Cycle Trader, an illustrated newspaper featuring classified ads and road tests, Buzz Walneck, publisher. Contact 7923 Janes Ave., Woodridge, IL 60517.

German motorcycle magazines
Markt fur Klassische Automobile und Motorrader. Huttenstrasse 10, D–6200 Wiesbaden, West Germany, or in the United States contact the Deutsches Motorrad Register, 8663 Grover Place, Shreveport, LA 71115.

Das Motorrad and *Motorrad Classic.* Leuschner Strasse 1, D–7000 Stuttgart 1, Germany.